KEEPING OUR HEADS ON STRAIGHT

✧

Journal Writing in the Golden Years

**Edited by
Eleanor Balaban-Perry**

CHICAGO SPECTRUM PRESS
EVANSTON, IL 60201

©1996 by Eleanor Balaban-Perry

All rights reserved. Except for appropriate use in critical reviews or works of scholarship, the reproduction or use of this work in any form or by any electronic, mechanical, or other means now known or hereafter invented, including photocopying and recording, and in any information storage and retrieval system, is forbidden without written permission of the editor.

CHICAGO SPECTRUM PRESS
1571 SHERMAN AVENUE
EVANSTON, IL 60201
1-800-594-5190

Printed in the U.S.A.
10 9 8 7 6 5 4 3 2 1

ISBN: 1-886094-46-2

To Baby Idney

My special thanks to Ray Wentworth for his cheerful readying of the text on the computer.

My gratitude to my friend, Oliver Andresen, whose words were the catalyst that spurred me into this editing effort.

It was my daughter who made this project possible by finding ways to conserve my energy. Thank you, dearest.

–*Eleanor Balaban-Perry*

CONTENTS

Commentary by Consensus vi
Introduction vii
Preface viii
൭ Klaus Ollendorff
    Bible Lore 11
    Hangover 12
    Never without 13
    Color Me What? 15
    Television Anonymous 16
    Splendid Brass Bed 17
൭ Minerva Bell
    Ambition 19
    Dear Walter Kelly 20
    Marvin 23
    Marcy 24
    Imperfect Specimen 27
൭ Oliver Andresen
    Gramps Jr. 30
    Magnificent Talk 31
    When Did the Universe Begin 33
    A Kiss of Dust 34
൭ Jackie Selig
    Mom's Funeral (Sort of) 39
    Joy 42
    Reset 43
൭ Leopold T. Rozycki
    The Good Deed That Wasn't 46
    A Bit of Trivia 48
    A Woman of Some Competence 50
    Small Business 53
൭ Ray Lewis
    Who Is Killing Johnny? 57
    Maxwell 58
൭ Carl Meyerdirk
    Growing Old Gracefully 60
    Psychic Solutions 62
    Irish Connections 64
    Stormy Weekend 65
    Acapulco 67

- Jane F. Jackson
  - First Try 70
  - Basseting 70
- Inez Boler
  - The Year Has Grown Old 73
  - I Write a Letter 75
  - Hard Rock Beat 77
- Marta Melcher
  - One for Me and the Rest for You 79
  - A Little Red Wagon 80
  - "Mist" 82
- Frances J. Markwardt
  - Baby 84
  - To Climb a Ladder 84
- Raymond Wentworth
  - Early Times 86
  - Meet My Parents 88
  - How Gilbert & Sullivan Changed My Life 91
  - A Tale of Two Trees 93
- Elaine M. Sheahan
  - Nosediving the Clipper 96
  - Stranded on a Country Road 99
  - a Senior's Weekly Journal 102
- Eleanor Balaban-Perry
  - I Come Out of the Closet 104
  - The Rest of Me 106
- Julia C. Attwood
  - The Feminist Movement and Me 110
  - Oops! I'm Grounded 112
  - Casting It Aside 114
- Jim Merrill
  - Red Is for Danger! 116
  - Granny and the Goose 117
- Joey Goldsmith
  - What Time Is It, Anyway? 119
  - Will Wonders Never Cease? 120
  - The Grass Is Always Greener 121
- Roselyn K. Wozniak
  - Action Near the Mailbox 123
  - Huey 124
  - 12600 S. Torrence Ave 126

COMMENTARY BY CONSENSUS

There are those who say we are in our golden years, but most of them have yet to arrive at that yearpost. When they start living those years, they might not consider them quite so richly colored. Fortunately, we have found a way to give some accuracy to the sobriquet. We mine our gold by journal writing. We think we have hit paydirt. After reading what we have to say, we hope you agree. We are not professional writers, but we are beneficiaries (that is most of us are) of a democratic education; some have gone further, but that basic schooling has enabled us to express ourselves in words sufficiently readable in syntax that scans. So we write the years away.

On the whole we are a jolly bunch, even those of us who have not been spectacularly successful in terms of material acquisitions. We have survived with long fruitful lives and have come to terms with what was meted out to us. For those experiences that are tinged with sorrow and disappointment, we have found their flip side, and that gives us strength and understanding.

Read and enjoy. Perhaps if you are approaching the golden years, you will try writing and becoming a journal head yourself.

–The Journal Heads

INTRODUCTION

Imagine yourself at a large gathering of witty, urbane "life travelers," each of whom has a story to tell. Imagine, during this party, you have the pleasure of spending time alone with each of its fascinating guests, people who, during the course of the evening, reveal a few adventures from their colorful and varied lives.

With *Keeping Our Heads on Straight: Journal Writing in the Golden Years,* Eleanor Balaban-Perry invites you to attend such a fete. In this collection you will find a number of brilliantly written encounters—some painful, some playful—each a vivid gem of insight and observation. Although every episode stands alone, the collection of unique voices and experiences woven together gains a sense of poignancy and power that elevates it far beyond what one normally thinks of as journal writing.

For several years, Ms. Perry has led an assortment of writing groups for the Chicago Department on Aging's Renaissance Court, located in the Chicago Cultural Center. In these groups, Eleanor has inspired, encouraged, critiqued and challenged a wide array of personalities and talents; the contributions in this anthology are offerings selected from these weekly classes. She and fellow members are to be congratulated on their dedication as well as their accomplishments.

If there is one basic truth to be gleaned from these writings, it is that life has its ups and downs and that somehow each of us has what it takes to cope, to move forward, to "keep our heads on straight."

–Larry Wallingford
Director of Program Services
Chicago Department on Aging

PREFACE

Keeping Our Heads on Straight is a unique collection of journal entries by an exceptional group of Chicago seniors who have gathered on a weekly basis to put their wisdom and experiences into words that can be shared with others. At each of our sessions, I delight to see my "journal heads" come with manuscript in hand. Some of their musings are scribbled on yellow legal pads, others are typed on ancient machines; a few upstarts among us even use a word processor. My instructions to them are tailored to inspire them to write and not be intimidated by those sneaky inner voices that question whether they are even capable of writing.

I say: write. Write as if you were chatting with your best friend or a close member of your family. Write in prose or, if it comes to you, in verse. *Keeping Our Heads on Straight* is the result of such simple direction. I have broadened the perimeters of journal writing, making it perhaps more contemporary, giving a place for fact and fiction, prose and verse. The results are heads and hearts working together with some therapeutic overtones. Such writing often reveals the secrets of the heart; it is a confessional without an inhibiting priest's presence. This is not an academic approach, but it is in keeping with the populist milieu of the times. Many of the writers, though unpublished, are good storytellers and aspire to write their family histories. Often children are too busy or bored to listen to a parent's reflections on the past. But when the parents are no longer around to give voice to these "boring repetitions," their children will be grateful to have their written recollections. These words, on the printed page, are a concrete legacy in black and white.

Journal writing is good therapy. In writing things down, we allow the sluice gates of memory to release the guilt and regret that lie buried in our consciousness. *Keeping Our Heads on Straight* is not literary, but it is delightfully readable and emotionally satisfying. These musings come from the heads of people who find themselves out of the mainstream by aging's inevitability, who are now people on life's back burners and have the time and inclination to reflect, to meld their understanding of today with their experiences in the past, and to share it with others.

–*Eleanor Balaban-Perry*

ɛʊ Klaus Ollendorff

BIBLE LORE

My mother's sister left Germany in 1934 and settled in Chicago where her husband had been invited to head the radiology department of Mt. Sinai Hospital. They lived in Hyde Park, and after his death she moved to a small apartment on Harper Avenue. Her greatest worry was the inability to get a visa for her father (my grandfather) to come to the United States.

One day in 1940, a few months before Italy's entry into World War II, a Bible salesman by the name of Stefani knocked at my aunt's door and made his usual selling pitch. My aunt told him she could not afford to buy a Bible and that no amount of prayer could help her anyway. Asked why, she explained that her 80-year-old father was trapped in Germany with no way to secure a U. S. visa. Mr. Stefani asked for a few details about my grandfather, which my aunt supplied; she also gave the salesman her telephone number. Mr. Stefani said that he might be able to help her and then left as poor as he had arrived.

A few days later my aunt received a call from Mr. Stefani asking if she could arrange to be in Washington in two days. He explained that his former minister, now chaplain to the U. S. Senate, had spoken to Cordell Hull (then secretary of state), and Secretary Hull had expressed interest in my grandfather's plight. My aunt was dumbfounded, grateful, and frightened. She called and asked me to go to

Washington in her stead because her English was not good enough. Of course, I agreed to go.

Lo and behold, two days later, I found myself in a huge office, at the far end of which sat the white-haired and distinguished Mr. Hull. He asked just a few, benign questions, personally jotted down my answers, shook my hand, and said he would let my aunt know if anything could be done. Within a week, a cable had gone to my grandfather saying, "Please present yourself to the American Consulate in Berlin for clearance prior to issuance of an American visa.." The State Department had arranged for a visa and for my grandfather to be met at the Brenner Pass railroad station (the border between Austria and Italy) by a representative of HIAS (Hebrew Immigrant Aid Society). The representative accompanied him on the train to Genoa, where he boarded one of the last ships to leave Europe for the United States. My aunt and I met him on arrival in New York, and I drove all of us to Chicago.

My aunt, though tearful with gratitude and full of invitations to Mr. Stefani and his wife for tea at her home, did not, to the best of my recollection, ever buy one of Mr. Stefani's Bibles.

HANGOVER

On New Year's Day I woke up with a hangover. Not from wine but from too much gossip. A businessman I've known for years told me that he would soon be filing for Chapter 11. A brand-new acquaintance confided her entire life history, including two divorces from incredibly hostile and stingy men. I was told about the illnesses of two friends and the sexual meanderings of another.

But the most unusual story I heard was about a recent wedding in the suburbs. Evidently the bridegroom had begun, just after the engagement was announced, to suspect his fiancee of a sideline love affair. Being a man of action, he hired a detective agency to have her shadowed. The agency quickly verified his suspicions and added that the beneficiary of the young woman's favors was Harry, his friend from schooldays and designated best man. The future husband could hardly believe the report, so he demanded photographic proof of this betrayal—and got it. A camera was hidden in his fiancée's bedroom, and it soon provided graphic evidence of her extracurricular activities.

So the bridegroom-to-be planned an act of revenge unsurpassed by any libretto of a Verdi opera. He went through all the usual prewedding celebrations and the ceremony itself. He placed the obligatory kiss upon his new wife's lips and ate his way through an elaborate dinner, complete with several toasts. As the celebration wound down, the new husband took over the microphone and said that he had an announcement to make. "I invite each of you to look on the underside of your chair where you will find a photograph of my wife, taken last week in her bedroom," he said. "You will notice that she is in bed with Harry. I invite all of you to keep the picture as a memento of this evening. And," he added, "at each table, one of the dessert plates has the letter 'A' on the bottom. The lucky user of that plate may take home the floral centerpiece. The 'A,' incidentally, stands for 'Annulment,' which I will seek tomorrow."

I believe that this story is true. I don't know what happened to him, to her, or to Harry. But the tale made such an impression on me that it kept going through my head throughout the first few days of the new year. Since there is no Alka-Seltzer for a gossip hangover, maybe my writing it all down for you will relieve my queasy feeling.

NEVER WITHOUT

I am the product of a childhood spent in Germany with a highly educated father whose pessimism was so great that one of his favorite phrases throughout my childhood was, "A good home is better than precious ointments and the day of death than the day of one's birth." (I learned much later that this happy phrase came from the book of Ecclesiastes.) In contrast, my mother's optimism was refreshing and encouraging. Humor was everything, and she much preferred to hear an amusing story from school than my memorization of the table of chemical elements.

Before hiking in the foothills of the Sudeten mountains, my father would tap the barometer, furrow his brow, and suggest that we postpone our excursion until the needle pointed to a more favorable position. My mother would go outside, see some blue sky, and get us all going. As the hike began, my father would warn me against running uphill, to prevent an early coronary, while my mother said, "Oh, let him go." My father would also use the hiking time to conjugate Latin verbs and practice hexameters. This was no doubt very informative, but the only one I remember is "Optimus cuncti sit tibi terra levis" (let us wish that we shall rest in peace). Other admonitions from my father included: no schussing because my skis would not stop in time; no racing bikes because of the likelihood of spinal curvature; and a two-hour wait after eating before going for a swim.

As you might imagine, this background has had its results. I have become sufficiently optimistic to attend a seminar like this one. But I also remember that when I bought a ticket to see *Hamlet* some years ago, I was convinced that Maurice Evans would become ill and his part would be played by a stagehand.

When I left Germany my father gave me several hundred condoms—which in a way showed unusual optimism—and he admonished me never to be without one. He even took to signing his letters "Nie ohne" (never without). My mother's optimism, on the other hand, makes me draw to an inside straight and laugh when I lose. Her happy outlook makes me hope each time I see the movie *Love Story* that Ali MacGraw will recover while watching Ryan O'Neal skate in Central Park. But still I am sure that Charleton Heston will lose the Ben Hur race. As I write this, I know that Purdue will beat Northwestern next Saturday.

COLOR ME WHAT?

After returning from lunch at Mitchell's, where Kate had a multicolored Greek salad while I had a small stack of pancakes covered with dark brown maple syrup, I began to wonder why she had been animated while I was morose. What could have caused this difference in behavior between us? Usually we are equally talkative or silent, pleasant or provocative, and often normal.

At home I found my German *Little Handbook of Food* (a volume of 1094 pages); no help there. Then—next to it on the shelf—I saw Ortega Y Gasset's book about European landscape and history, *Stern und Unstern* (Star and Nonstar). I found Gasset's theory about the different behavior patterns of Mediterranean people and North Europeans. North Europeans, who are exposed to greens, grays and blues, are more sedate, slower; the farther north you go, the more depressed and suicidal they become. In contrast, Spaniards, Italians, Greeks, Turks, and all others who are exposed to the bright yellows and reds of their environment are sanguine, noisy, fast-moving (when not sleeping), and life-affirming.

Could people who were born in a Chicago suburb or in a Central European province be affected by colors? Or what about Kate's Greek salad vs. my drab pancakes? Perhaps. The Hispanic busboy was so fast that he cleared the dishes from the table as soon as Kate had put the fork down, and then hesitated when he saw my brownish-looking plate, which he left there until we departed.

I began to wonder what the dominant colors of Pakistan are. So many cab drivers go through red lights. Would a more neutral color prevent accidents? Ortega does not mention for how long one would have to be exposed to either color dominants before a change takes place. Do people who spend their winters in Scottsdale become more optimistic? About the Cubs? Do they begin to feel red instead of blue?

What is the significance of the green gowns worn by operating-room personnel? Do they calm the patient and reduce the amount of anesthesia he needs? And is the green card for immigrants supposed to have a soothing effect? Would a red card instead inspire feverish job hunting?

I am beginning to feel blue about writing this and, if you aren't, there must be too many bright colors in the room.

TELEVISION ANONYMOUS

Last week I was in bed with the flu. In contrast to Marcel Proust, who wrote his great books while lying in bed, I watched television. A new world as it turns with all my children entered my life. Soap operas are full of intrigues, conspiracies, illnesses, and requests for forgiveness. Why do I stay with this?

I began to feel guilty. Proust in my condition remembered significant feelings about his mother, wrote them down, and achieved everlasting literary fame. I lay there and also thought about my mother. I thought she would have advised Freddie not to take out Beverly because Kathy had told him that Beverly hated to cook. This fleeting thought made me switch to *The Frugal Gourmet*, a maniac with garlic. He was making me hungry. Off to the refrigerator, then back to one—no, two—Spanish-speaking channels, each with its own tele-novella.

When I found that Juanito seemed to be advising Frederico not to take out Esmereida, I switched again, and tried my hand at *Jeopardy*. I soon found that the only thing I really knew was where Proust had written his *Remembrance of Things Past,* and found myself shouting, "What is bed?"

Every channel had news at five o'clock, and each featured winsome little jokes between the male and female anchorpersons, sometimes with the aid of the weatherperson. Then the weatherperson warned us of terrible storms due to hit Chicago. What can I do about that? And why do paid reporters thank other paid reporters for doing their jobs?

My mind began to atrophy, and I have come to class today to have it reprogrammed. It may not happen because I keep worrying about Ralph, who might set fire to his brother's building in order to persuade Lily to marry him. And what if Steve goes to Burma to shave or to find Bertha who had vanished before her finals at Bennington?

I need Television Anonymous before it is too late.

SPLENDID BRASS BED

For most of February, Kate and I rented a small apartment on the beach at Longboat Key, Florida. As we walked on the first day, I experienced a flashback to childhood, rare for me in such an American landscape. My heart sank. There in the bedroom stood a large and splendid brass bed. There in my mind I was back at my eighth birthday, the day I told my great lie and my mother told her tiny one.

A month before my birthday, my uncle showed me a new bed frame he had bought for his mother, my grandmother. Like the Florida one, it was huge and resplendently brass. I declared that bed to be the most beautiful in the world. My uncle agreed, explaining that it was a golden bed and adding, "Some day I will give you one just like it." I hoped, perhaps felt sure, that the someday would be that soon-to-be-reached eighth birthday.

On the day itself, my teacher asked me to stand up in school. The teacher, whom I loved, called me Froeschl, "little frog," for the bright green sweater I often wore. "Froeschl," he said, "tell the class what gifts you received today."

"A golden bed," I replied.

"Surely not," said that practical man.

"Yes," I insisted, "I got a beautiful golden bed."

After that, the school day went on in the usual way and I almost forgot about my wishful lie. Next day, a Saturday, many of my classmates and the teacher arrived at our house for the customary birthday party. Each child was given a cap of Indian feathers, raspberry juice, and cake. Soon all of us were restless to go to the backyard and slay the white man.

"Just a minute," said my teacher, "I am sure everybody here is as anxious as I am to see your golden bed." I took off my Indian gear, hoping to become a paleface and drop dead on the spot. I looked at my mother.

"Mutti," I said, "Don't you remember that Uncle Arthur promised me a golden bed?"

A slight pause while I gazed with pleading eyes at my upright and honorable mother.

"Oh yes," she lied. "I hope it will be delivered before the party breaks up."

So she saved me and turned me into a lifelong loving son. What she couldn't foresee was the uncomfortably restless nights I would spend some seven decades later in my golden bed in Florida.

༄

Klaus Ollendorff, an escapee from Hitler's Germany, is now a retired businessman, and delights the journal "heads" with his comic twists of circumstances as he writes of the foibles of our times.

∽ MINERVA BELL

AMBITION

I was never a professional performer, but I had ambitions and dreams in that direction ever since I listened to "Hot Stuff Jackson" and hoped that some day I might host my own radio show. I gave recitals at my church, appeared on programs at neighborhood festivals, made guest appearances at other churches, and entered and won oratorical contests. I did everything I could think of to gain experience as a speaker. (Hadn't John H. Johnson written in my high school graduation book, "To Minerva, the best actress I have ever seen."?) I was known to have clear diction, to use good grammar, and to handle myself well in all areas of public speaking.

Later, when I was 20 years old, I saw a newspaper ad that I thought might be an avenue to realizing my ambition—an evening class in radio broadcasting at DePaul University. I registered for the class, paid the tuition, attended several classes, took notes at the lectures, and prepared the required assignments. None of the other students (they were all white) ever said anything to me, and the teacher never addressed me until the time came for the first speaking assignment.

When I opened my mouth to speak, the instructor loudly interjected: "What? What? What on earth are you trying to say? I cannot understand a word you are mumbling! Be seated! You will never make it in this class!" In a state of shock, I crept back to my seat. When the class was over, I left the building and never returned to be further humiliated or to try to get my money back.

This took place just prior to World War II. The Fair Employment Practices Commission had not yet come into existence. Dr. Martin Luther King, Jr., had not yet delivered his "I Have a Dream" speech. Attorney Elmer Henderson had not yet won his lawsuit against the railroad for discriminatory seating practices. Jesse Jackson had not begun to speak up for the likes of me. Thurgood Marshall had not won the suit against "separate but equal" educational opportunities. I read about the NAACP in the *Chicago Defender* newspaper, but I did not know of anything that could have been done about what had happened to me at the words of that bigoted male Caucasian.

Now, 50 years later, I still wonder why he felt so threatened by my presence—whether it was my being black or female or the volatile combination of being both black and female!

DEAR WALTER KELLY

September 18, 1995

Dear Walter J. Kelly:

I was one of the many excited people who attended the Retirement Dinner last evening at the Beverly Country Club. I was personally acquainted with five of the ten retirees, and was the student of four of them. I only came to the dinner because I wanted to say "Thank you" and "Good-bye" to you and Sherwood Snyder.

Many nice things were said about you, and I know that you have been the inspiration and the instigator in the lives of thousands of your students, each of whom has his own story. Let me tell you mine.

The very first course I attempted at Chicago State University, called "The Chicago Experience," was an extension seminar course taught by Professor Walter J. Kelly. In my evaluation of the course I described it as "quite a delightful experience—a most painless way to learn and to expand one's horizons."

We met on Saturday mornings at the Florence Hotel on 111th Street in the Pullman Historic District. There we heard many exciting and informative lectures and discussions. Sometimes we took excursions into various ethnic neighborhoods and parts of Chicago. The Pullman area was one of them.

The whole semester is now a blur of exciting activities. Never in my life have I so looked forward to Saturdays. One especially memorable Saturday, Mr. Albert Logan came to discuss one of the subjects on our class outline: "The Black Experience; Some Special Problems." This was made more special to me because he chose a subtitle: "From DuSable to DePriest." Since I graduated from DuSable High School and had my first NYA part-time job performing clerical duties in the office of congressman, orator and statesman, Oscar DePriest, I felt sure this lecturer came for my very own benefit! (By the way, your friend Mr. Albert Logan died last week and the funeral mass was held at St. Edmund's Episcopal Church on the same day as the retirement dinner.)

One Saturday, we visited a Greek neighborhood and enjoyed a wonderful Greek meal as a part of our educational experience. The wonderful bread, cheese, and the special wine completed a very special day.

Thanks to you, I attended my very first matinee at the Opera. The opera was *Rigoletto* and it was made so special to me because I had worked in that building during the early WWII years, but it had never occurred to me that I could be a part of another world.

Most exciting of all, however, we spent all day one Saturday on the water. You and Mrs. Kelly and some of your children picked me up at my home. The chairman of the geography department made us a part of his annual tour. We boarded a ship in the north branch of the Chicago River. We sailed through the locks into Lake Michigan and took in that marvelous view of the Chicago skyline. We proceeded all the way south, under the 95th Street bridge, continuing to the Sag Canal. There, we turned right and proceeded west until at some point, we turned north again and reentered the city through its backdoor—seeing the back of the Civic Opera Building, and back again to the Wacker Drive launching place.

The geography department chairman kept us enthralled as we again absorbed knowledge in a completely painless way about the history and the geography of Chicago—when and where different ethnic groups entered the city, how certain boundary lines (railroad tracks, street car lines, bridges) helped to form the boundaries for neighborhoods.

I wrote a paper for the course entitled, "What Happened to the Three Presidential Candidates of the Class of 1936." In it, I delineated how I fit into the class outline. You complimented the paper, gave me an "A" and urged me to register in a degree program. You even offered to sponsor me in whatever plan I chose.

Later, you enabled me to gain some extra credits in history by sending me an article from *Dial* magazine which gave me a subject for my major paper, "Changing Images," which was published by a neighborhood newspaper.

I want you to know that my whole life has been immeasurably enriched because you opened up a whole world of the love of learning to me. I am sure you knew that I received the bachelor of arts with honors in 1983. I am not sure that you know I was awarded the degree of master of arts (English) in 1990, eight years after I had retired from working at Chicago State. The graduate division presented me its academic achievement award in recognition of superior scholastic achievement.

Now, in case you and Mrs. Kelly wonder what old folks like me do with their time, I am presently enrolled in a journal writing class downtown in the Chicago Cultural Center. We are writing our life stories, just as you hoped I would do when I wrote that first paper for you in 1976. I am also honing my skills at my IBM Personal Computer. I was 76 years old on September 12, 1995, and I'm so busy. As they sang in the old Negro Spiritual, "I Ain't Got Time To Die!"

I hope and pray that your retirement years will bring you good health and much joy.

Please tell Mrs. Kelly that I still delight in her recipe for zucchini with tomatoes and oregano (to make the kids think they are eating spaghetti).

Yours very truly,
Minerva Bell

MARVIN

When my son Marvin was a little boy, he had trouble with the letter "L." He pronounced it like a "Y." That is, he talked about "c-y-iming" up on the "yadder" to fix the "yight," the way Daddy did.

When he entered kindergarten, I went in to meet his teacher to let her know that we were aware of the problem, and to say we would register him with a speech therapist if she so recommended.

The tall, slender, blonde lady greeted me and I said, "This is Marvin, and I am his mother, Mrs. Bell." She responded, "I'm glad to meet you." Then, with a decided lisp, she added, "I am 'Mitheth' Kirby."

We decided not to mention the speech therapy at that time.

We also stopped nagging him and let him go on saying his table blessing, "John 3:16. For God so 'yoved' the world that he gave His only begotten son and whosoever 'beyieveth' in him shall not perish but will have 'ever-yasting' 'yife.'"

We also let him go on singing his favorite song, "How could you 'beyieve' me when I said I 'yoved' you, when you know I've been a 'yiar' all my 'yife.'"

We didn't even remember when his "Y's" turned into "L's." When I mailed a card to him for his 48th birthday, August 21, 1995, I signed it, Beyieve me, I yove you with all my yife.

MARCY

Marcy was one of the secretaries who worked with us in a large deparment of the university. She worked doggedly at whatever task was assigned to her.. She could be depended upon to complete any chore in a timely manner. She worked grimly and determinedly. There was no nonsense about her.

Most of us were of her generation and we were all hardworking women, but we were not beyond joking or having some fun in the process. Marcy frowned at some of our frivolity, and we often wondered whether her disposition was what the Bible meant by "Blessed are the poor in spirit . . ."

A student wife who once worked with us referred to Marcy as "the kind of woman who, when she was a girl, if she had a rocking horse, it died." She really did not mean to be unkind, and we really should not have laughed our silly heads off, but we never forgot the statement.

Every one of us was working, either to pay off a mortgage or to put children through the University Lab School or college. Marcy had only one daughter, but she was also supporting a husband through graduate school.

All of the secretaries were neat and clean. Some of us shopped in the university thrift shop, but Marcy looked like she shopped in the thrift shop. Her skirts, her hats, her coat—everything she wore was too old, too large, or too, too, out of fashion.

Marcy seldom went out to lunch with us to celebrate birthdays. The leftovers she brought from home for lunch looked "tired" and very unappetizing. We saw bread that was much too crusty, cheese that was just this side of moldy, and fruit that was well past its prime. She explained that she always put the best pieces in her daughter's and her husband's lunches. Sometimes, we saw her push aside greenish discoloration from cottage cheese.

In all the years we worked together, only once did we have a group meeting at her home. None of us will ever get over our first sight of the tastefully furnished and beautifully decorated apartment. Not one of us would have thought that she was the mistress of this lovely home. There was nothing outmoded or secondhand. We decided that this lovely, immaculately clean and stylish apartment was maintained so her husband could be proud to entertain his university colleagues in it.

Our secretarial staff was like a miniature United Nations. Our origins were from every corner of the world. Marcy was of Italian descent, but she was singularly the least stylish of us all. Someone made the snide remark that if all roads lead to Rome, none of them lead to Marcy.

Many of Marcy's lunch hours were spent doing research to assist her daughter or her husband. We had an excellent library in our school, and because of her skills, she was able to be of great assistance to the students in her family.

All of us have retired from working at the school now, but some of us still exchange Christmas cards these many years later. We still shake our heads in pity and shame when we hear from or about Marcy.

Most of us have long ago paid off those home mortgages. Our kids have graduated from college, and most of us have

Keeping Our Heads on Straight

moved on to other pursuits. None of us secretaries ever struck it rich, but our labor did help our professors achieve their goals.

No occasion is more elegant than the pomp and ceremony of a summer commencement at the university. Neighborhood children and many people from all walks of life line the sidewalks to see the colorful procession into the university chapel. All of us watched when Marcy's husband strode proudly past us into the chapel to receive his Ph.D.

We fully expected that when Marcy reported to work that next Monday morning, by some miracle, there would be a beaming smile on her face over her husband's great success. She was more grim than ever. It was a long time before we got the news.

Marcy's husband had told her he really appreciated all she had done for him. He told her that she really should have received an equivalent degree. He said, "Marcy, you have been a wonderful helpmate, and I do really love you in a way. But, at this point in my life, I want to strike out in a new direction. I will be leaving shortly to accept a position at Indiana State University. When I am settled, I expect to help support our child. Now, with me out of the way, you can concentrate on taking better care of yourself."

More than 30 years have passed since we worked together, but I thought of Marcy just the other day when I heard someone read a few lines from Maya Angelou's poetry:

"My life has been one great big joke
A dance that's walked
A song that's spoke
I laugh until I almost choke,
When I think about myself."

IMPERFECT SPECIMEN

No matter how diligently they search, most girls never meet Mr. Right. Instead, when they receive a marriage proposal from "Mr. Almost-All-Right"—with stars in their eyes they begin to sing, "Aisle, Altar, Hymn." Of course, they mean, "I'll Alter Him."

Take me, for instance. If the good fairy offered to perfect that "specimen" I married, how would I respond? Because, imperfect specimen, indeed he is.

He never puts the toilet seat down, and often leaves a ring high up in the bath tub. But on the other hand, there is much to be said about my own imperfect specimen.

At a teen-age club party where I first met him, he asked me to dance. I thought he held me just a little too tight as he called out to his friend, "Eddie, how do you think MINERVA BELL sounds?" This provoked leers and laughter from our assembled friends. But here we are, three children and three grandchildren later. expecting to celebrate our 54th wedding anniversary this year.

My mother did not like him, and went out of her way to discourage him, but he kept coming back. Even after we married, she was cold and distant to him. Even when she lived in his home, she criticized and did much to disparage his every effort. But he never raised his voice in anger to her. It should be noted that she did not like the men any of her three daughters married, not the doctor, nor the postman, nor the serviceman.)

In the World War II U. S. Army in the United States and in Europe, he was a very good soldier, excelling athletically and academically. He rose through the ranks to become the top noncommissioned officer in his company in a four-year enlistment. There were no bad marks on his record.

He did not earn his high school diploma, but after his honorable discharge from the army, he returned to his job at

Roberts & Oake and worked there steadily until the stockyards closed in Chicago.

Several odd-jobs later, he obtained employment at the American Maize Corn Products Company and worked there for 17 years until mandatory retirement at age 62.

He projected an excellent father image, even though he was not always anxious to take us to the zoos and amusement parks we clamored after because of the strange hours and shifts he had to work. But his children and his family could depend on him to do whatever was necessary to build and maintain a very stable family. By his own good example, the children learned to do the honest and honorable thing.

Even though he grew up in a very rough part of Chicago, he never used foul language. Many of his friends would use the oath, "Jesus Christ!" when angered, but our kids knew that Walter's strongest oath was "Cheese an' crackers!" whether he smashed his finger with a hammer, or stubbed his toe while carrying their fish aquarium full of water and a dozen swimming creatures.

We played many table games; Scrabble was the family favorite. We encouraged this game because it forced the children to do some mental arithmetic as they were building a vocabulary. Even now that there are no children at home, we still play Scrabble every night. Some of our friends have an alcoholic nightcap before going to bed, but the two of us try to win two games out of three before we hit the sack. We find this so stimulating and we keep learning new strategies to improve the game.

After we both retired, we became better companions than ever before. He developed several new interests and I developed different ones. He never tried to dissuade me from what pleased me. He often shook his head in wonder because these took us in many different directions. He became a trophy-winning bowler and swimmer; I finished college.

Walter knows that I do not like to do housework and he does not bug me about my much-less-than-perfect housekeeping. In fact, from time to time, he will pitch in to help keep the place presentable. He does sometimes gently remind me that I am a pack rat and need to get rid of excess paper and books.

We do have a number of interests in common, too. We sing together in the church choir. We completed a course in square dancing and received a diploma. We joined a club where we dance every week.

He is not demanding about food preparation. Whatever I fix is okay with him. Also, he will take me out to dinner a couple of times a week if I like.

I have kept writing to get to the part where I would tell the good fairy what should be done to perfect my spouse, but I have come to the conclusion that he is a much better spouse than I am. I think I should leave well enough alone. In fact, instead of buying him a birthday card this year, I think I will give him this article for his 78th birthday, April 30, 1995.

Minerva Bell could be called a late bloomer. She received her bachelor of arts degree at 65 and her master's at 70. She dances square, round and line, and keeps a journal while harnessing the computer.

ଔ Oliver Andresen

GRAMPS JR.

"Come on, now, I'll get you a dog," said Cliff's grandfather, "but not one of my Labradors. They're special."

"But Gramps, that's why I came with Mom to Wyoming. So you could give me a dog," said Cliff with tears on his face.

"And so I will. I have a neighbor who has a beautiful female registered collie. She was all set to be bred when she—well, let's put it this way—she eloped. Now she's the proud mother of six scroungy little mutts. For five bucks I'll get you the pick of the litter."

"But Gramps, I want one of your dogs."

Gramps scratched his skinny neck. "Come see Patsy," he said. "Then maybe you'll understand."

Behind the house was a shiny-clean kennel. Gramps knelt and pushed back the burlap curtain over the door. Cliff knelt beside him and peered into the darkness.

A soft growl greeted them at first, but was soon followed by the slapping sound of a welcoming tail. A heavy black Labrador lay on straw, patiently waiting to bring forth new life. In the darkness her eyes glowed like flaming candles through black velvet.

"How's my girl?" whispered Gramps, reaching to pet her head. "She's due now," he said softly to Cliff. "Isn't she beautiful?"

With wide, dry eyes Cliff stared at the large, black animal. "Yes," he said quietly.

"Her pups will bring me a thousand dollars apiece. That's why I can't let you take one back to Chicago."

His lips tight, Cliff nodded.

"After all, to a kid a dog's just a dog," said Gramps, letting the burlap curtain drop back in place. Then he stood up.

But Cliff stayed on his knees staring at the burlap curtain.

Gramps scratched his neck while staring down at the boy.

Six weeks later, Cliff and his mother began the long drive home. In his lap Cliff held a happy, wiggling black Labrador pup.

"That was nice of Dad to give you such a valuable animal," said his mother. "What are you going to call him?"

"Gramps," said Cliff.

"But he's just a baby."

"Then I'll call him Gramps Jr.," said Cliff. "After my grandfather."

MAGNIFICENT TALK

On nights when the stars are particularly close, I remember Mr. Grimstad. He was the father of my friend Fred Grimstad, when we were young boys. In those days I could hardly consider Mr. Grimstad as my friend. I was too much afraid of him. He had a tremendous temper and would scatter the entire neighborhood gang like rabbits when we fought or cried while playing near his house.

I remember one Saturday afternoon I accidentally shut the front door on Fred's hand and made him scream. Fred and I were just fooling around and didn't realize his father

Keeping Our Heads on Straight

was listening to the Minnesota-Michigan football game. Mr. Grimstad came out of the radio room like an enraged bear. He didn't touch either of us. Frankly, he never put a hand on anyone in anger. But he kept us cowering in the kitchen for three-quarters of an hour while he kicked furniture and threw things against the walls. We always took the trouble to walk softly and to talk of pleasant things when Mr. Grimstad was at home.

Yet, he had a liking for me. I guess I was particularly quiet and comfortable for him to have around. Besides, Fred and I liked to listen to Mr. Grimstad talk. Never since have I heard such magnificent talk.

After a day that had been peaceful or a dinner particularly pleasing, Mr. Grimstad would lean back in his leather chair by the fireplace, stare at the smoke from his cigar and tell us about all the things he had done or had read. His particular interest was astronomy. When he began to talk about the stars, Fred and I would sit on the sofa with our knobby knees to our necks while our imaginations rode through space and time on Mr. Grimstad's mind.

One night he explained how the speed of light had been determined by a star peeking from behind the earth's shadow on the face of the moon during a lunar eclipse. The sun is so far away, he said, that its hot light takes nine minutes to reach the earth. So great are the distances in the universe, many of the stars we can see have burned out long before the earth began—their remaining light just now reaching our night's sky.

"How big is the biggest star?" I asked.

He laughed and said he didn't know, except that the sun is a star big enough for a million earths to fit inside. Yet, the sun is a small star.

"Then what's the smallest star?" asked Fred.

I remember Mr. Grimstad answering that no one could possibly know—that perhaps atoms are little stars and planets. All matter, he said, is made of little planets whirling around their tiny suns—and so infinitesimally small and close together that things seem solid to the touch. At that, he reached over and thumped the bricks of the fireplace with his fist and an understanding of the atomic theory leaped into my mind.

Mr. Grimstad seldom went to church. Like most blustery people, he was really very shy. He complained that when he sat in church, people would always turn to him and stare. And yet, on that particular night, Fred, who was looking through the window at the stars over Lake Superior, asked, "How could anything be so big and so far away?"

"And how could anything be so small?" I asked, frowning at the bricks of the fireplace.

"God," said Mr. Grimstad and he laughed softly for a long time. "There is God."

I shivered when he said that. For that one moment I felt I knew everything.

WHEN DID THE UNIVERSE BEGIN[1]

If the universe began
    what was before the beginning?
If the matter composing the
universe occupies space,
    what is beyond the space?
The only reality is change,
    ever changing unlimited
    matter in the now.
As for the purpose?

[1] Reprinted from "Letters to the Editor," Time Magazine, 3-27-95

A KISS OF DUST

"Ashes unto ashes, dust unto dust—oh me, oh my!" muttered Olga, dabbing a lace handkerchief to her ancient eyes. Mr. Norstad, the kindly local farmer, and his two husky sons, had finally managed to raise Father's coffin from the grave.

"What's that, dear?" asked Ada, younger than Olga by 18 years, but still shriveled and bent with age.

"I was recollecting the funeral—oh, so many, many years ago," said Olga. "That was supposed to be the end of it, you know. But now the whole town will say it was my wits gone cockeyed again to have this done."

"Oh I can remember the day," said Ada. "But what else are we to do under such disconcerting circumstances?" From her black-beaded bag, she drew out a tiny handkerchief to press against her quivering, pale lips.

It was before the turn of the century. The Milwaukee Railroad planned to reach up through Wisconsin from Chicago to the Twin Cities and it would pass by the small town of Medford. As a matter of fact, it would run right through Medford's old cemetery, with the northbound tracks passing right across Father's chest.

Having spent all their very long lives in Medford and in somewhat reclusive circumstances, the two sisters' thoughts of both the quick and the dead held equal prominence in their minds. So now what's to do about the Milwaukee Railroad's running over Father? The only solution, of course, was to move him to a new family plot on the safer side of town.

So now, on this very hot day in June, Olga and Ada were having their father disinterred.

Their father, a shrewd merchant, had been a Scandinavian of the old school. Because of his encouragement and support, his six sons had each left home at the age of 21 to scatter themselves throughout the world. Two of the boys—

who had abstained from excessive alcohol—had become men of distinction.

But Olga and Ada being female, their father had considered them a lesser species. Consequently, for them all questions concerning the practical matters of life must be left entirely up to him. As a result, the two women had never been educated, married, nor traveled much beyond the confines of Medford.

While the Norstads, with grim and sweaty effort, hoisted the casket into the back of their horse-drawn wagon, Olga got an idea. "Why not take Father home again—just for the afternoon?" she said.

Ada concurred. "A lovely idea," she said.

Mr. Norstad resisted their request at first. But Olga had a certain strength. Also, she offered to double their fee. So the two sisters' father, on his way to his second final place of rest, was dropped off first at his former place of residence.

Ada hurried ahead into the house to put two chairs before the great stone hearth for the casket to rest on—just as it had done so long ago. Olga stayed behind to make sure the Norstads did not jar their burden or inflict any other undue damage to disturb Father's repose. The Norstads were then instructed to return and complete their mission later in the afternoon.

With the casket in position before the fireplace, Olga drew the shades against the hot afternoon sun. Then she and Ada took their seats midpoint in the room. With their hands folded in their laps, they exchanged smiles in the semi-darkness while the June bugs snapped against the window screens. How nice to have Father home again, they said.

The Olga got another idea. Fortunately, wrapped in brown paper on her closet shelf, she had kept Father's old slippers. She would fetch them now and put them on the hearth as he had liked to have them so long ago.

"My, how we'd scurry about when we heard Father's footsteps on the porch to make sure his slippers were warming before the fire," she said. "As a matter of fact, we always scurried at the sound of Father coming home regardless of the weather."

Ada, in turn, remembered that in her top drawer behind her jar of attar of roses was Father's old pipe. She would get that, she said, and put it on the mantel just as he used to do.

"Of course, the pouch is gone," she said as she gently tapped the pipe against the chimney to free it of old ashes and dust. "Mother burned the pouch along with the rest of Father's tobacco the morning after he died. Remember how we all hated the stink of his smoking so much? Still, it really didn't matter, of course. Father, as a man, had a right to his pleasures."

After completing these new arrangements, they again seated themselves. Olga sat tall, pale and radiant while Ada sat slumped in her chair, flushed and somewhat shaken with all the excitement.

Then with a whisper, Olga offered another suggestion.

"How nice it would be to see Father again—just one last look," she said.

Ada touched a handkerchief to her eyes. "Oh one last look indeed would be very nice," she said.

And so Olga crossed the room to the casket. Very gently she began to work at the latch. There was a hissing sound as air returned to the casket's interior after having seeped away over the years. With a click she lifted up the lid. Lo! There was Father—just as he had been on that final day so long ago. How peacefully he rested in his dark suit with his soft, white hands positioned across his chest.

Unbeknown to the sisters the moisture in the new air began to swell the desiccated molecules of the corpse.

Olga took her seat again. But now she was frowning, her eyes flicking back and forth from her father's long, artistic fingers to her own rough-skinned hands in her lap—hands so mercilessly scarred by so many years of menial labor about the house and farm. As a matter of fact, her attention to her hands now brought to mind the memory of her mother with her hands at final rest on her chest in her casket some years back.

But Ada continued to smile while wiping her eyes in the darkened silence. And now she had a suggestion.

"Let us give our father a final tribute," she said.

When Olga asked what she had in mind, Ada replied—"a kiss"—although she would have the courage only if Olga went first.

Olga hesitated. Finally she rose and slowly crossed the room to the casket's side. With tightened lips she peered into the face of her father—the stern face with the great Scandinavian nose and high forehead that still portrayed his intractable will. Wagging her white-haired head, she slowly bowed to press her lips to his.

A shiver distorted her aim. Instead of lips pressing lips, the tip of her large Scandinavian nose touched his.

At the twinkling of an eye, the face of her father collapsed, unveiling a leering skull. With a vocal gasp, Olga grabbed the coffin's edge for support. The resulting vibration continued the disintegration. In the very next moment, their father had crumbled away to just a skeleton lying in tattered black cloth and dust.

With a screech of a gull, Ada fainted dead away to the floor.

But Olga stood tall by the casket to stare at the ruined remains. For a moment she was silent. Then she chuckled. With a new intake of breath, she barked a laugh. Then, throwing back her head, she roared with laughter—a rasping cackle as raucous and shrill as from a witch in hell. Only after a stirring moan from Ada on the floor did Olga contain herself.

"You needn't have tarried so long," said Olga to the Norstads when they returned.

Speaking in hushed tones for the occasion while maneuvering the casket towards the door, Mr. Norstad asked, "Will you and the other missus be following us to the new grave, ma'am?"

Olga replied with a strong voice. "I think not. My sister is resting—and I have new plans for my evening. The caretaker at the other cemetery will show you where to go."

Olga followed them onto the porch. With the casket out in the sun, Mr. Norstad noticed that the latch had been disturbed.

"You didn't go to open it, did you, ma'am? I doubt you was supposed to do that," he said.

"No matter to you! Just get it away from here!" said Olga crossly.

As the Norstads gingerly carried their burden down the front steps, one of the boys leaned back his head towards Olga.

"Hey lady, how'd he look?" he asked with a wink.

He blushed at the fiery, icy glare Olga gave him in return—but then glanced back again at the confounding sparkle in her eyes. Her withered lips hardly moved to answer.

"Not so brisk," she replied.

☙

Oliver Andresen, professor emeritus, says "Kiss of Dust" is a true family story which he has recorded in his journal for posterity. Morticians have corroborated the "dust" facts.

☙ JACKIE SELIG

MOM'S FUNERAL (Sort Of)

The call came about 10 A.M. She introduced herself as policewoman something or other. "I'm sorry to have to tell you, but your mother was found dead in her apartment about an hour ago. We think she died about 4 A.M. Can you come to Florida today to make the necessary arrangements?"

Have you ever walked into a door by accident? I felt as though I had done just that and my chest had been the point of impact. She had been found fully dressed with shoes on and hair combed on her way to the kitchen. Dead of congestive heart failure. Mom never wore shoes at 4:00 A.M. I knew she had prepared herself to die.

My sister and I were on the next plane. As we flew I remembered the other plane trip when I took Mom down there for her move. Here she was, in her seventies, uprooting herself for a new life where the warm sun might ease the pain she lived with daily. She was so afraid of flying. Neither of us were drinkers, but I got the stewardess to give each of us a drink and we settled in to play gin rummy for the length of the flight. The drink seemed to mellow her, so I asked for another. Before long neither of us cared what card was played. Any card was an excuse for hysterical laughter.

It was a shock to be handed a taped cardboard box by a somber funeral director. Could this little box contain the remains of a human being? He assured us that it did, accepted my check, wished us well, and his look said he had to get on to his next customer.

That was the beginning of my grief process. Disbelief! Oh no, it can't be!

I had already decided what to do with Mom. As my sister flew back to Chicago, I left to put Mom where she had been the happiest in her youth, that small town in the mountains of Pennsylvania. My daughter met me in Philadelphia and my cousin took us back to Lansford to set Mom free. I packed some of her things in a shopping bag, being careful to put the box in the center to protect it. Suddenly, I felt a terrible agitated nervousness as though the bag was about to explode like Mom wanted out of that bag. She had always been somewhat claustrophobic. I dived for the box, and so help me, once it was in my hands my agitation disappeared and I was calm once again. I held that box in my hands from then on, making myself a promise not to put it anywhere. When I boarded the plane for Philadelphia, I was dead tired from the packing. I knew I might fall asleep and drop the box.

I did the only sensible thing: I told the stewardess what the box contained, how tired I was and my concern that the box be safe. She looked at me suspiciously and then decided I wasn't kidding and said, "Well, here, Hon, let me put the box securely on top of your bag and we'll strap the bag in a first class seat where it won't be disturbed."

I had to laugh. The first person in my family to fly first class was my dead mother and she didn't even need a ticket.

I met my girls in Philadelphia where we spent the night. Lindy, the youngest, was in trauma, this being the first loss she was old enough to really understand and feel. We went to the prearranged hotel and on the pillow of the bed in our room was a note from my older girl Jan, "Down in the cafe—neat band to dance to."

Well, that might sound bizarre to some, but I guess she is my daughter all right because to me Mom's death wasn't sad. It was freedom from pain and being alone more and more as her friends became less mobile. It's okay in my book to dance at whatever occasion I consider happy. Lindy thought Jan was pretty awful, but then there are eight years between them.

In the morning my cousin drove us up from Allentown and we decided to show the girls where I had spent the happiest days of my life when we visited Mom's family every summer. My cousin had Frankie Carl and the Ray Coniff singers on his tape deck. I swear I felt a peace I hadn't experienced in years. Oh yes, the box was firmly in my hands as we drove to Coaldale to see Grandpa's store where Mom was a girl. And then on to Lansford to see the store her sister and family owned where I was allowed to make boxes at age six, keep the perpetual inventory from sales tickets at age nine, and help the coal miners' kids steal coal for their own stoves at home. There I learned about John Lewis's attempt to unionize the miners and free them from the vicious ripoff of the company stores. That was the Depression, but I don't remember a happier time even though Mom told me later that one day my dad came home, threw a nickel on the table and told her that was all they had in the world.

The girls enjoyed the tour, but then it was time to do what we had come for. Cousin Leon drove slowly on a back highway while we searched for the perfect place, a secluded, shady glen with wild flowers growing in profusion. Mom loved wild violets.

"Stop, Leon, you just passed it!" I yelled at Leon, who was lost in Frankie Carl's tinkling piano. Oh, what a spot we found. As we walked toward it, Jan and I sang loud choruses of "Always" and "Let Me Call You Sweetheart," Mom's favorite songs. Lindy was there, too, about ten feet behind, head down, shuffling along and definitely not singing. There it was: the spot, a floor of wild violets and other flowers in the shade of huge old trees, and beyond, a valley surrounded by rolling hills bathed in sunshine.

Leon said, "I'll stay in the car." (I understood his devotion to Frankie Carl.)

Jan and I wished Grandma a safe trip while Lindy watched in horror as we opened the box, sprinkled the ashes among the flowers and threw the box in after them. We got back in the car, sang one more chorus of "Always," and that was the end of our celebration of a courageous lady's life.

After lunch at Leon's house, Jan went back to Minneapolis, Lindy and I flew to Chicago. I knew then and I know now, I loved my mother and she loved me.

JOY

I saw the movie *Kids* and came out so "down" that I wanted to cry for these babies whose lives are already over because of liquor, drugs and unsafe sex, and they're only young teens. It started me thinking about my own childhood, and I zeroed in on about eight or nine.

My days were spent playing with other kids like myself, children of fathers who stayed with the same company forever (or so it seemed), mothers who were there to see us off to school with hot cereal and a glass of milk to make our bones grow strong. That's what they told us, but really I think it was to make them feel needed. They were there when we came home, to supervise the change of clothes and the snack to give us the energy for our let-the-games-begin-empty-lot-Olympics. Some of these snacks were, from this vantage point of distance, a bit strange. In my neighborhood the favorite was rendered chicken fat spread on white bread enhanced with bits of chicken skin and onion that had been fried to a fare-thee-well sprinkled on top. The more grease that poured down our forearms as we ran out the door yelling, "thanks

Mom," the better to attract dust in the empty field, where for endless hours, we played house, cowboys and Indians, baseball, or just dug holes to sit in and talk.

We talked of how unfair life was to a kid. "What did we know," was what everyone said to us. We talked about the need to remain independent and not believe everything those grownups told us, and what we were going to do with our nickel allowance for helping with the dishes and keeping our room fairly neat. We plotted the assassinations of our siblings and, of course, we dissected the weekly serial episode at the neighborhood movie house and wondered if our hero would make it through another week. I figured out that there would be no serial if the hero got killed off, but I kept this insight to myself; I enjoyed the amateur screenwriters' efforts to extricate our hero. During these talking sessions, it was fun to look up at the sky and watch the clouds move and change color as the afternoon wore on. (That is still one of my favorite sports.) We caught bugs and let them go and wondered how squirrels remembered where they left their stash.

Then came the inevitable raising of apartment windows and mothers' voices calling roll as they summoned their next generation home. The first call was the alert, the second was "I mean business," and the third was "get yourself in here or else," and we knew our day in the world was over. No one wanted to find out what "or else" meant. Tomorrow would be the same; every day brought new excitement, new plans, new hopes for kids' rights. It was a continuation of what went the day before, but to us there was no sameness to it—just pure joy.

RESET

Looking up at the red digital readout
As the machine went click, click, click,

I knew I was sick,
Sicker than many times before.

As I drifted off to sleep
The digital readout stopped showing numbers
And gave out urgent messages

Reset, reset, reset,
Or my poor abused veins wouldn't get the needed
infusion of four different meds
On the piggyback I.V. stand.

We can put men in space with style and grace, but
We can't put an I.V. in to stay in place
and keep on going
Click, click, click.

That's when you know you're sick;
You control nothing at all.
It's an effort to flick the switch and ask for help, and
Yet you must.
The thought of giving up is scarier than the message,
Reset, reset, reset.

God, this night never ends
As the machine delivers and sends and I,
The least important part of it all, wait for the nurse to say
It's time to replace this infusion profusion,
Again.

Don't tell me about your wonderful I.V. skill. Be still.
Find the vein that doesn't roll from others, you mothers,
That under skilled fingers swell proudly to say,
"I'm here dear,
Plunge the needle in and success will be yours."

Reset, reset, reset.

Re-stick, re-stick, re-stick.
I don't want to be this sick.

ల

Jackie Selig, wheelchair bound, finds her creativity and spirits soar when she writes. Besides journaling, she edits a newsletter for one of Chicago's intergenerational housing facilities where she lives.

❦ Leopold T. Rozycki

THE GOOD DEED THAT WASN'T

When you get off the subway train at the Lake Street stop and follow the crowd past a spot that is always wet, which you hope is not the river trying for an encore flooding, an escalator will take you up to within a few steps of the State of Illinois Building. Through a turnstile is a lower-level rotunda with numerous fast-food places. On the open floor area are many white plastic chairs and rather nice looking granite-topped tables. An unlikely combination that suggests to me a lady in a full-length coat wearing gym shoes, white gym shoes.

 I had got into the habit of getting coffee and a doughnut at a place that calls itself the Randolph Street Market. Their food choice ranges from Spanish, soups, salads and bakery goods. After paying at the counter that has a wide access on either side, I would take my tray to one of the tables close to the walking aisle where I could watch the people walking to and fro without a thought of Michelangelo, unless he was a cement contractor on the city payroll. As I sat with my coffee, I watched a stocky person in a trench coat walk to the kiosk that contains the garbage cans. He pulled open the gate and began to rummage through, apparently looking for some scrap of food. He had no luck so he moved on, scanning the tables for anything edible. No one paid any attention to his scavenging.

As I sat sipping the coffee, I could see what appeared to be another scene in the ongoing soap opera of the real world. Down the aisle, toward the Randolph Street Market, a man dressed as a construction worker might be was coming my way. He carried a container of coffee. At the counter of the Market, the cashier was walking around in circles as if in distress, looking at the man with the coffee. From all the signals, I deduced that the man had got the coffee and walked past the cashier without paying. My deduction may have been right. A security man appeared and stopped the man with the coffee. The three—man with coffee, security man, and cashier—were in some kind of discussion. At this point, I thought why don't I get in on this scene and try to create some kind of diversion. A little bit of bluffing, perhaps?

I got up, walked over to where the group stood. When I got closer, I could see that this might not be easy. The fellow with the coffee was more frowzy looking than I realized, and a dragging shoelace didn't help. However, as I got close, I said loudly and vehemently to the guy with the coffee, "Where the hell have you been? I thought you were right behind me."

He blinked, maybe out of nervousness. The cashier and security man looked a bit startled. I continued with my lying explanation. "We work for the same firm and today it was my turn to pay for the coffee. I thought he was right behind me." The security man looked skeptical. I took out a dollar, handed it to the cashier, and asked, "Will that cover it?" She took the money and was happy to have done with the matter. For the benefit of the security man, I said in a confidential manner, "He lost his wife a couple of weeks ago and it has been hard on him. That's why he looks like a bum."

"Uhhuh," was all he said.

Then I grabbed the man's arm and said, "Let's go, Joe," and walked him away along the aisle till we were halfway around that circle of eating places and out of view of the security man. "Are you hungry?" I asked. He nodded, "A hamburger?" He nodded again. We moved to read the menu on the wall. I told him, "Get what you want, I'll pay." He ordered a cheeseburger, french fries, and a milk shake. He took the food to a nearby table and sat to eat. He was hungry. I stood there, not very politely, watching him eat.

He looked up at me and said, "I suppose I should say much obliged for the break. My name ain't Joe, it's Pete. But you stuck your nose in where you shouldn't have. I wanted the security people to hand me over to the police. Then I might have been taken to the station, thrown in a cell, and probably got to sleep inside plus have meals for a couple of days. So you didn't do me any favor getting me out of that spot. Next time save your do-gooding for little old ladies." And he went back to wolfing down the food.

This was an aspect of the matter that had not occurred to me. "Well, better luck next time," I told him. And I left. I could have given him that line from Burns, "The best laid plans of mice and men gang oft agley," but I'm sure he knows it and anyway he wouldn't appreciate the thought or the poetry.

Funny thing, next time I stopped there for coffee, the cashier asked if my friend had adjusted to the loss of his wife.

I said, "Huh?"

Then I remembered. "Oh, yes, he is getting a little better," I said. I suspect she knew what I was up to. Women can be perceptive that way.

A BIT OF TRIVIA

When the temperature goes to uncomfortable in the high digits and lingers there, my memory bank clicks on, going into reverse to another time, another place.

The average temperature was 100 degrees, but this was a hot spell and for some weeks the temperature fluctuated between 110 and 120 degrees.

This was the California desert 15 miles south of Yuma. Mexico was 10 miles further south; their name for the area was the Sonoran desert. This was our training area, which we shared with coyotes, jackrabbits, scorpions, and rattlesnakes.

A training exercise was conceived by the commanding general, who felt that hardening men to desert conditions was a matter of maximum exposure. This type of logic had made him a success at his previous stint. He arranged a game of find the food and water rations from map locations with given compass directions.

The first platoon that tried to do this got lost. They were out there three days without water. The air in the desert is like one of its creatures only much more evident. And deadly. It is like some inhuman thing out of science fiction, an unseen something that sucks the life out of human beings, just simply through their pores.

Three days into the exercise, some one may have told the general what could happen to men in the desert without water. There is no hardening effect; you die. A search was ordered. They found the platoon. Three men were dead, dehydrated, their bodies turning black. The remainder of the men were nearly at that point, but still alive.

There was an immediate but clumsy attempt at coverup. Time magazine picked up the story from the Yuma newspaper. Many letters were written, the bulk of them by mothers, demanding that the general be punished. The army quietly moved him to another area.

Mistakes are made; the bodies are wrapped in a flag and buried. But how do you explain to the boy's parents that it was all a mistake made out of ignorance?

A bit of trivia was contributed by a barber, when we were moved to Fort Dix for transhipment. His remark, "Where in the world have you guys been? Your hair is so dry it breaks off, like part of it is dead."

A WOMAN OF SOME COMPETENCE

My way of coping to arrive at normality after a period of distress over a personal problem was to take a course at the local college. I chose to get into a photography class, as I had some familiarity with that subject. It needs saying that it was a good, effective therapy. Simply associating with the young people, who generally were intent on getting the subjects and making the grade, did a lot to cheer me up. It was a restorative for the psyche and for my sense of humor.

As I got into the routine of attending, it became a habit for me to stop in the cafeteria for coffee or orange juice and a trifle of food. When the cafeteria was crowded, there would be company at the table. One of those times, I sat across from an adult, a rather nice looking blonde woman. In a school cafeteria there are no conventions for opening a conversation. What I came up with was, "You're here for a course?" You will note that this may be answered simply by yes or no or it may lead to more talk and it did. She was here to take the course in computers. In her job she was doing the payroll for what I gathered was a small but growing company, and she was anticipating the time when it would be done on or with computers.

We ran across each other a few times in the cafeteria. She seemed to enjoy talking. One time she asked, "You were in the war?" I nodded my head. She continued, "I had a lot of trouble during the war. I was in the Ukraine." She paused as if recalling. I looked at her with the Ukraine in mind. I thought that out of that area the people might have a trace of Mongolian features. Then I recalled that in the southern Caucasus was a people called the Circassians. Their women were highly prized for their blonde hair and white skin. These were negative assets, so to speak, in that this led to their kidnapping or outright sale into Arab and Turkish harems.

She continued her story. "All that fighting when the war broke out and food was hard to get, so I took my son and we went through all those countries to get to England and then to America."

In those few words she made it across Europe in wartime. I would guess that it took a high order of planning, connivery, subterfuge, and God-knows-what-all to manage that kind of trip.

"I have this house in Wicker Park. You know Wicker Park?" she asked.

Yes, I did know Wicker Park. It is a section of Chicago with a corner at Damen and North Avenues that has been designated as an historic area. Some of the early settlers in that area, industrious Germans, put up solid, substantial homes of fine baked brick. The interiors had fireplaces that were lined and faced with imported tiles and marble. The interior wood trim was beautifully carved mahogany and walnut. A Swedish group put up a church in the area. They had the architect design the interior to suggest or resemble the inside of an old time sailing ship. Up the street, on North Avenue, an old building still has signs on its front, announcing that Turkish and Russian baths are available, also massages. That is—were available. Now it is boarded up and, like all boarded up structures, is being vandalized. The neighborhood is changing. Not far from the church, a multiple-family building was remodeled into condominiums. Recently in one of the condos, a woman was killed in a home invasion.

To get back to the blonde and the story she had to tell.

"My son had gone to California for a vacation. I was alone in the house. Then the outside yard light burned out. It was located high on the side of the building so I could not replace it. It worried me, because I had read about the woman who had been killed just a few blocks from me. I slept poorly for a few nights.

"Then one night, it was toward the early morning, I awoke. I thought I heard something downstairs. I got up, went to the dresser where I had a pistol. I took it out, walked out of the bedroom to the head of the stairs that leads to a downstairs hallway.

"In the little light that comes from a window, I saw the figure of a man. Was he coming in or going out? I could not tell. I carefully aimed and shot. Then I went back to the bedroom and called the police. They came very quickly. I had to go downstairs to get to the door to let them in. I pointed to the intruder and they checked. He was dead. They called an ambulance to take him away. Then I had to go to the station to help them make out a report.

The captain at the station was very angry. "'Did you have to kill him?' he asked.

"He made me feel that I was the criminal. A policeman came in and whispered in the captain's ear. I heard a little; the man had a record. But I was treated badly. Maybe the police felt that I was taking away their job, doing their work for them."

She certainly was indignant about the bullying she got at the police station.

Suddenly, I had a flash of insight; it became clear how she managed to get across Europe in wartime. It was the shot. Shooting downward in dim light at a dark figure, the odds are against you. To kill a person under those conditions, you have to be a very good shot with a pistol. It was easy to see that men who stood in her way or thought that here's a nice blonde to spend some time with, just couldn't read the fine print, like maybe, "hazardous to your health," may have discovered too late that under that blonde hair was a black widow spider. The thought struck me as funny and I grinned.

"Why you laugh?" she asked. Sometimes she lapsed into that alien twist on English.

"Oh," I said, "it's just that the police are always like that."

"Well yes," she said, "he only yelled. In Europe it was much worse, very bad. Now I feel better. I think no one will bother me."

My thought was, oh boy, you can bet on that. Thank goodness the school term is coming to an end, and I'll not see this lady again. Now don't get me wrong. I am all for ladies defending themselves, but a pistol can be so terminal.

SMALL BUSINESS

Everyone has at some time used the expression, "I knew them when;" when they were going together, when they got married, when they split up, etc. Sometimes the I-knew-them he or she may mean that the person has moved on in life into a different level of society as a result of having done well in the stock market or whatever. The ambition and drive that put them there often shows up at an early age. That was the case with Tony.

Tony and I went to the same school and we became friends. One day Tony came to the house to see me. He had come across a great money-making idea. He showed me a small ad he had cut out of a magazine. "Make money raising earthworms" was the heading, and the ad went on to say that it took very little time or care, just some dirt and the worms would do the rest, that is, multiply. Then they might be sold to fishermen as bait.

I didn't think it such a great idea, but Tony kept harping on it as a moneymaker, so finally I said "Okay I'll go in with you."

"They want three dollars for a starter kit. I've got a dollar." Tony said, "Maybe you could make up the other two. That way you will be the majority shareholder."

And that started the business.

Nearly three weeks later the mail had a package with my name on it. The return address was Live Earth Productions. Opening the box, I found a cardboard container like the ones the delis use when they sell potato salad and the like. And when I took off the lid, there they were—the worms.

Right away I called Tony on the phone. "Why," I asked, did you have the worms sent to me?"

"Well," he said, "you've got a bigger yard and I think your dirt is better."

I accepted that. "But what am I going to do with them now? The ground is still frozen."

"That is a problem," said Tony. "What if you just put them in your freezer for now?"

"But, but—"

"I know what you're thinking, Freddie, but they'll probably go dormant like bears that sleep all winter."

I was doubtful, but I said, "All right, I'll do that." I was glad Mom wasn't home as I wasn't sure how she would feel about worms in the freezer.

When Mom got home, after a hello, she said, "Freddie, tomorrow you are going to have to drive me to the eye doctor for my checkup for new glasses."

"Okay Mom, what time?"

"I have to get there at four o'clock. It's a bad time. Then we have to rush home so I can make supper for your father. Think I'll make spaghetti."

After school the next day, we did that. Mom got those drops in her eyes that make your eyesight worse than it is, but she got busy making supper, while I started on my homework. I could hear her talking to herself in the kitchen, and I should have listened to her saying she knew she had part of a container of hamburger in the freezer that she could use for the spaghetti sauce, but I was concentrating on the algebra. When Dad got home, Mom dished out the spaghetti, ladled on the meat sauce, and we ate.

"By Golly," Dad said, "this is a delicious meat sauce, best you ever made!"

Mom was flustered at the compliment and started to tell how she had been lucky in finding the leftover hamburger.

A light bulb went on in my head, and to myself I said, Oh no, it can't be. I got up from the table and looked in the freezer. Yes, the container of worms was gone.

"What are you looking for, dear?" Mom said.

"Ice cream," I answered, "but I don't want any now."

Then I went to the phone to call the biology teacher. Any problem—he had told us. Well this was. I explained the situation to him. When he stopped laughing, he said, "It's no big deal, no problem at all. Your Mom cooked everything and, as a matter of fact, worms are eaten in quite a few countries. Rich in protein." He was laughing as he hung up.

Next I called Tony and told him the worm deal was off.

"Why?" he asked.

"We ate them."

"Why did you eat them?"

"My mom thought they were hamburger."

Tony was indignant. "If you ate them, I want my dollar back for my share of the worms."

"Just try to get it," was my reply.

That ended our friendship, and shortly after Tony and his family moved away. I never saw him again. Some years later, I saw a printed photo that looked like him. It was in the post office and a short bio alongside it also mentioned, "Wanted for embezzlement and mail fraud." It might have been him?

To this day, I have as little as possible to do with worms.

☙

Leopold T. Rozycki: "What do I get out of the journal writing class? Most important is the meeting itself and the communication between members. The written material from the past, made readable, hopefully interesting, is at least as enjoyable as doing the crossword puzzle. The effort to remember, the energy spent in writing is an exercise at the primary source that gives the good feeling that follows physical exercise."

ಛಿ **RAY LEWIS**

WHO IS KILLING JOHNNY?

Who is killing Johnny, and making him so he cannot read?
Every time I hear of it, it makes my heart bleed.
Kill him, lock him up, starve him, if you please—
Of all the cures put forth, a few are these.
Where do you stand when Johnny does not meet the goal?
Are you there to help, or do you fold?
Johnny used to be a little lad, two, three, or four;
Now Johnny has grown up—you can't handle him any more.
If you are not careful, Johnny will get sore;
You call him a dummy; when you send him to the store,
Then you expect him to act smart.
You always bawl him out, but you never take him to your heart.
You are always pointing your finger at someone else you see,
When maybe you are the culprit—the buck stops with thee.
You go around, as smug as smug can be, saying everyone is guilty but me.

You tell yourself a lie,
You give yourself a clean bill of health; please tell me why.
What did you do for Johnny, when he was a lad,
When Johnny was four or five, and without a Dad?
Did you try to help him, tell him what to say?

Or did you tell Johnny to go away?
Johnny was on the dole, they needed money there—
Did you act to pay your tax to try to keep him there?
Or did you howl, loud and long, tell him to get out of your hair?
When he came to school feeling bad,
Did you try to find out why, or did you just get mad?
He is grown up, now, and ignorant as can be.
He's big now, big enough for anyone to see.
He feels so awkward listening, but not to understand.
What are you going to do with such an ignorant man?
Is Johnny lost? I'm afraid he is, for time waits for no man.

MAXWELL

In my third grade class there was a lad.
He was always good and never bad.
I had an argument with this kid,
I do not know why, I just did.
We decided to fight after school.
I knew to tackle me he must be a fool.
We met outside to have our spat,
I knew I could beat him, because he was fat.
Fat guys are sluggish, and cannot last.
He cannot beat me, I'm too fast.
We just had a billowing snow,
This only made my blood flow.
He put up his dukes, I put up mine,
I thought I'll lick him, and I would feel fine.
I rushed at him to end his case;
I ended up with snow in my face.
I rushed again to show I was tough;
In the snow again, I knew it was no bluff.

Ray Lewis

I had pride, I had ego,
If you bet on me, you lost your dough.
I thought to myself, this is not right,
He is doing me in, and I can fight!
I threw an awful right at his head;
I knew when it landed he would be dead.
Down I go, in the snow again.
Doing this to me was a sin.
I fooled around, I started to bluff,
This fat guy was pretty tough.
I must end this fracas in some way.
I certainly rue this day.
I never thought with my ego,
I would end up in the snow.
I said, This time I'm going to let you go,
I guess you won't tangle with me no mo'.

You know, he never did!

Ray Lewis, who writes verse and prose, says, ". . . I believe to correct anything you must start at the bottom and work up . . ."

☙ Carl Meyerdirk

GROWING OLD GRACEFULLY

Florida is more a mental attitude than a geographical location. Occupied by a large number of geriatrics—at least during the winter months—its restaurants, its newspapers, even the predominant body style of automobile, have been affected by these residents.

A Sarasota south side restaurant that's always packed from around 11 a.m. until midafternoon is the Old Original Oyster Bar. I'm not sure that oysters are ever on the menu, but there's a daily cocktail special available for $1.55. Each day a different drink is highlighted, giant Margaritas or daiquiris or whiskey sours. After you've become pleasantly and economically tipsy, for only around another $3.39 you can alleviate the pangs of hunger with a luncheon special. A mug of your choice of spicy red fish chowder or Boston-style clam chowder can be followed by fried grouper fingers, French fries, and cole slaw or any one of a dozen other selections including grouper nuggets, ocean perch, catfish, crab cakes, stuffed shrimp, and the like. Everything is fried, and everything is accompanied by French fries and cole slaw, but the snowbirds from Ohio, Michigan, Illinois, Nebraska, Indiana, Minnesota, and central Canada love it.

The parking lot is jammed with their great gas-guzzling behemoths. A friend believes that Florida should replace the 50 special vehicle plates it now issues, honoring everything from the manatee, the panther, and Cape Canaveral to its university athletic teams, substituting only one that reads "Land of Lincolns." Town Cars come in every shade and vintage, usually carrying five ladies with perfectly-combed hair and driven by a sixth, the smallest of the group, who alternately looks just above the rim of the steering wheel and through the spokes as she pilots the car down Highway 41.

The newspapers also devote a lot of space to the special interests of the elderly. On a recent Sunday, Sarasota's *Sun-Sentinel* allotted most of its feature section to exploring the cost of eternal rest. Its other readers and I now know where to order a booklet with instructions for making our own coffins for $9.95. We also learned about the process of mummification and that the best technicians are Florida-trained. We discovered that a company exists that will deep-freeze your remains for a mere $120,000.

However, to prove that its editors also realized that all oldsters weren't quite ready to shuffle off, another day the paper devoted a feature to listing 50 things—from sex to illness resistance—that get better with age. On St. Valentine's Day, there was the touching story of a couple from small Michigan towns about 100 miles apart who had first met on simultaneous senior trips sponsored by their respective high schools nearly 50 years ago. They finally married—after their first spouses died—after 40 years without contact. They light candles at every meal, when they eat out. Must be a real jaw-dropper at McDonald's!

But the most awesome statistic was that this year 76 million of what we used to call Baby Boomers will begin to hit 50 at the rate of one every 7-1/2 seconds. That means that people who not too long ago were staring at Lava Lamps, smoking dope, and listening to Iron Butterfly will be entering—uh—well, they've even come up with a new term for "middle age." In the future, it'll be called "mid-youth."

LensCrafters, the eyeglass conglomerate for the common man, has gone one disorienting step farther. No conversation about "middle age" or even "mid-youth" in their corporate corridors. Instead, they refer to "presbyopes," which I finally found defined as "far sighted." This major shift in demography is certain to have an enormous impact on advertising and product spokesmen. Envision with me Michelle Pfeiffer pitching Arthritis Pain Formula and Sharon Stone with Depends.

PSYCHIC SOLUTIONS

My first-floor tenant in the north building is the financial vice president of a company that does business in a number of international locations. A couple of months ago, as he was departing for a 10-day trip to Milan, he asked if I'd mind looking in on his cat—a mature calico with the demeanor of Queen Victoria—during his absence. I agreed, and the cat and I got along fine for the duration of his absence; she'd meet me at the door to the apartment each day and escort me to the room where her feeding bowl, water, and litter box were all arranged. I'd put some fresh Meow Mix, "now with ocean fish flavor," in her bowl, and she'd begin nibbling genteelly, punctuating the bites with monosyllables of kitty conversation. After eating her fill, she'd never fail to climb on my lap for a brief "purr" of gratitude. She had excellent manners. Then she'd climb down and walk to her rug to resume her nap. I had been dismissed.

Early this month when my tenant departed for Ankara, he left a note with his rent check asking if I'd serve as cat-sitter once again. I anticipated no difficulties, so I didn't even try to contact him. But this time has been different. At each visit, Queen V seemed increasingly agitated. She declined to dine. She walked around the rooms emitting little sounds of distress.

After two days when this disturbing behavior was repeated, I called the man's secretary to ask if she knew the

Carl Meyerdirk

name of the veterinarian. Of course she didn't, but she suspected that he might be somewhere in the south suburbs, where the tenant had lived formerly.

That avenue closed off, I cast around for other options and remembered that I had once read of an animal psychic, who had reported near miraculous results in treating everything from a sick three-foot iguana with a liver ailment to a tarantula, who had confessed to a weakness for playing practical jokes on children in a classroom.

One of her bits of wisdom was about flies that people had asked her to remove from their barns. "Flies are very instinctual," she said. "You can talk to them, but they're not going to listen."

A consultation with this expert in sensual phenomena was reported to be $25, but she had made the mistake of disclosing too much about her methods to the reporter. She had said that she mentally asks the animal 10 questions, including what makes it happy and unhappy.

I decided I could employ the same methods and save myself a fee. "Okay, Queen V," I said, "why are you dissatisfied?" staring deep into her almond-shaped eyes.

She wiggled and looked down at the newspapers at my feet. My tenant had failed to stop his daily newspaper subscription during his absence, and the papers had been piling up near the cat's sleeping rug. On practically every front page for several days there appeared a story about the candidacy of Pat Buchanan.

That's it! She's worried about the presidential campaign—and the distressing strength of a man who, when advised he should broaden the base of his campaign, supplemented his attacks on free trade and immigration with new ones on Buddhists, Jews, homosexuals, and welfare queens. I carefully removed all of the newspapers except for one front-page section that carried a big picture of Buchanan in Louisiana. That one I placed under the litter box.

That evening everything seemed normal. Queen V met me at the door, her regal bearing fully intact. Psychic analysis really works along with a can of Fancy Feast.

IRISH CONNECTIONS

"Have ye Irish connections?" is the question American tourists visiting Ireland are asked. And when I responded to our grey-haired host that family legend indicated that my mother's grandfather originated there, he nodded wisely and settled back in his chair.

"Well, I can't tell ye from where he came, but I can tell ye the road he took to leave."

I probably looked a trifle surprised, possibly doubting, as he continued: "It runs down to the old harbor and it was the same pathway taken by the millions who were forced to leave their loving homes and for a future they knew not what. It runs past a wall, and if the stones in that wall had tongues, the sad stories they could tell. Enough to make your eyes weep and your heart bleed and break."

I set my suitcase down and seeing that he had captured me, he leaned forward. "Let me give you a little history lesson. Now, I have nothing against the British themselves. We don't have finer people as guests in this house than the English are. But the British governments are a different matter. They took this country illegally by arms, and they've been determined to keep it at all costs.

"And what a bitter cost it has been to Ireland's people." His voice rose as his sense of outrage increased. "There was no need for the hunger and the people dyin'. There was plenty of wheat, but the British masters had control and they shipped it from the country as people lay in their beds starvin'.

"That wall to the harbor—it was built by slave labor, by Irishmen paid wages so poor they couldn't buy food for their families where there was food to buy.

"One poor man workin' on the wall had eight children and his wife had just died. Her sister had gone out before to America, to Boston or Chicago, and he knew that his only hope was to send the children out to her. As he worked, he watched his children walk slowly, weeping, past the wall toward the waiting ship, and he knew he was never to see them again on this earth. His heart grew heavier and heavier, but he decided he must see them and kiss them and hold them one last time. He left his work and went to the boat for the last farewells, but when he returned to the wall, there was no job for him. And he died three weeks later."

He sank back into his chair, watching my face closely. I wasn't sure how to respond and picked up my suitcase with a stammering. "Thanks for telling me that. It's very interesting."

As I walked to my room, I remembered a breakfast conversation with a young man from Downpatrick a few days earlier. I had remarked that the Irish seem to have a story for every circumstance. He agreed. "Sometimes they even believe them," he said.

I wasn't sure how much of the story of the wall was accurate history or how my host could have known such intimate details. If challenged, he would have said that the actual facts weren't important, that it could have happened. It was the sort of thing the British would have done. Points of view and politics have obscured facts and will make any settlement of the Northern Ireland problem difficult, if not impossible.

STORMY WEEKEND

The birds have been missing from the feeders all day, but now with heavy snow falling, evidently signaling the arrival of another Arctic front, they've appeared in great numbers and are feeding ravenously.

The showiest, of course, are the cardinals, the males in their bright scarlet cloaks. The females, feathered feminists, less gaudy and wiser of eye, seem to accept their flamboyant husbands with an air of tolerance. Amused indifference. But my favorites are the juncoes, hump-shouldered little Eastern European-grandmother birds, with their gray shawls pulled tightly around their shoulders, skittering around in the leaves beneath the bird feeder. At the finch feeder, filled with fresh thistle seeds just that morning, a quartet of purple finches fills every available perch, sitting motionless except for regular sidewise motions of their heads to choose another morsel from the cylinder.

The area immediately behind the house is an oasis of quiet, but beyond it in the distant backyard the wind off the lake is tossing the tops of 60-foot trees like giant eggbeaters.

There's a warm fire crackling on the grate. The logs, seasoned well by the warm sun during the dry summer, are burning brightly. It's a cheerful, comfortable scene. Inexplicably, my thoughts race backward through the years and across the miles to my childhood and even before that. My thoughts are as turbulent as the treetops. Why did my mother and father decide to marry? How did they meet? I'm sure if I asked my father that question, he'd respond that it was too many years ago and that he no longer remembered. Perhaps it's true. Perhaps at his age—almost 95—he does not want to cause himself the pain of remembering.

I can speculate. My mother was the third daughter in a family of six surviving children of a farmer grubbing out a meager living on an 80-acre hilltop farm. Her two older sisters were already married to neighboring farmers, and she was past 18 with no serious suitors. But she was comely—lively hazel eyes gazing out of a pretty face surrounded by softly waving brown hair. My father was the only son of a rancher, and doubtless he came calling in an automobile—one of the first in the county. He might have preferred to have ridden his horse with its saddle of hand-tooled leather, but how do you take a young lady for a ride on a horse? Certainly he would have worn his cowboy boots. His stepmother always said he was "small for his age," and fully grown he stood only 5 feet, 7 inches in stocking feet. His Hessian posture plus the heels of the boots would have made sure he could look mother straight in the eye.

Did they love each other? I can't recall ever hearing the word "love" in relation to another human being in our household. Family relationships—what they meant, how one acted—were simply understood. You didn't wave your arms around a lot and talk about it. You simply lived as everyone expected, respecting and obeying your parents, particularly your father, without questioning or examining your emotions.

Perhaps that's why a solitary afternoon leads to this kind of journal writing.

ACAPULCO

Evidently at a loss for a good subject for her column one day last week, Ann Landers had reprinted some signs found in foreign countries indicating the worldwide usage of and difficulty with the English language. Among them was one reportedly seen in Acapulco. "All water used in this hotel has been personally passed by the manager."

It's a good giggle, but I seriously doubt that it's of current date. Today the countless busloads of grandparents from Indianapolis and the Business and Professional Women's Clubs of Peoria flooding the area for visits of four days and three nights have encouraged most of the service people to speak better English than the residents of South State Street.

Admittedly, this wasn't always true. Some 25 years ago—and then annually for the next 10 or 15 years—a group of us used to fly from Chicago, Detroit, Pittsburgh, Kansas City, and San Francisco to rendezvous at Thanksgiving on Acapulco's beaches. First there was only one high-rise luxury hotel, El Presidente, near the center of the magnificent Crescent Beach, but that one was soon to be joined by dozens of other hotels and condominium buildings on both sides of the Avenida Miguel Aleman. Shoulder to shoulder, they extend in a line from the old morning beach at Caleta on the north to the sunset beach near the Hyatt on the south just before the road climbs upward into the hills. Merle Oberon used to live there, and the sister of Iran's shah, and Ireland's Guinnesses in a house next door to one once owned by Frank Sinatra. The area was called Las Brisas for the sea breezes that swept away any hint of tropic heat.

Down in the less rarefied area of the Costera, as the main boulevard was called, there were interests who wanted to expand the appeal beyond the international social set. Fiestas Americana, a one-time American Airlines subsidiary, purchased El Presidente and soon added two more hotels—the luxury Condesa del Mar overlooking Condesa Beach and on the land side the more plebian Fiesta Tortuga, named for the sea turtles. Soon after, someone erected beside the Tortuga a monstrosity named the Romano Palace to call attention to a line of concrete replicas of Roman statues that lined the pool area.

This was the time and probable location of Ann Landers's sign. The rapid expansion had left the service people more than a little unprepared. I remember one morning entering the American Airlines reservation office at the hotel to reconfirm my flight home, a requirement in those days. The lone clerk was speaking rapidly in Spanish on the telephone. Five or six people waited in a single line leading up to her counter. The conversation continued for several minutes when the clerk suddenly interrupted her caller with "Uno momentito." She placed the receiver carefully on the desk in front of her, turned, and moved toward a filing cabinet that she opened. From the cabinet she extracted a tube of hand cream; she removed the top and carefully and methodically spread cream over both her hands, massaging it carefully into her skin. Then she recapped the cream, replaced it in the file drawer, closed it, and moved back to the receiver. Placing it to her ear, she said, "Si?"

There was the time a friend stopped at Sanborn's, a drug chain that's now partially owned by Walgreen's. He settled at a stone-topped table on a terrace overlooking the Pacific and ordered a banana split. When it arrived, it was breathtaking in its beauty—three large scoops of ice cream, topped with chocolate, strawberry and pineapple syrups, and liberally garnished with fluffy whipped cream, chopped nuts, and not one but three maraschino cherries.

When he dug deep into the confection the first time, he missed the banana. Another spoonful and then a third and still no banana. He signaled the waitress, who came rushing over. "Si, senor?"

"I can't find the banana in the banana split."

"Oh, si, senor. Today we have no bananas," and turning, she walked away.

෴

Carl Meyerdirk considers himself a "69-year-old adolescent using journal and other types of writing to achieve maturity." Today, in retirement, he manages his own residential property and works pridefully in a large garden at his home in Lakeside, Michigan.

JANE F. JACKSON

FIRST TRY

I fluttered my eyes,
I made them twinkle
For all the old guys,
My charm I sprinkle.
Tea dancing at one
All seniors can come;
I danced when young
Now my limbs are sprung.

The rhumba I try,
My rump goes awry.
Hot cha-cha beats neat
But where's my feet?

Fun flirting is fine,
But won't work next time.
Guys, gimme a chance,
I wanna tea dance.

BASSETING

This Sunday, as most Sundays, I drove to Barrington Hills to hunt rabbits on foot with a pack of basset hounds. No guns, we chase the scent. The Spring Creek Basset Hunt meets Sunday afternoons at 2:00 p.m. to pursue rabbits through brush, bramble, woods, and creeks. Afterwards, the hunters, called basseters, enjoy a high tea and fine bourbon in various lovely homes in the area. There are only 1,000 basseters in the United States. We are elitist.

The hunt season begins with the Blessing of the Hounds—never, never call them dogs—on the first Sunday of October and continues each Sunday until the three-day celebration in April. The bash includes an invitational hunt with other packs throughout the United States. Coveted ribbons are awarded, as well as the Perpetual Trophy, a silver tray, engraved with the name of the winning hound and the sponsoring hunt club. A formal ball on Saturday night and an awards luncheon on Sunday conclude the three-day affair.

The blessing rite dates from medieval times when hunters sought the intercession of St. Robert to protect hounds, horses, and riders. Robert was a ninth century pleasure seeker whose chief delight was hunting, but after a dramatic conversion experience while hunting, he became a priest and eventually a bishop. Though he gave up the hunt, he is honored as its patron saint.

During our October blessing ritual, the minister blesses all the participants of the hunt, even the prey. The joy of hunting is chasing the scent; wild rabbits, however, know all the cover. I have actually seen a rabbit swim across a creek.

Clever rabbits can outrun the basset hounds. With their short, stubby legs, floppy ears, and low-slung bellies, the hounds often lose the scent and start running in the direction from which the rabbit came. They give "voice" or a distinctive bay. More or less controlled by a medieval horn, the sport engages huntsmen, whippers-in, a field master, and then the participants who are called the field. We stay behind the field master, not wanting to distract the basset's elegant nose.

Whenever a rabbit is spotted by the field, a loud yet restrained "tallyho!" and a pointed finger indicate the rabbit's direction. As soon as the hounds get the scent, loud excited baying starts. The field often completes an exhilarating hunt with shining red faces, spatters, and wet clothes—I once fell into a creek—and a great deal of camaraderie.

We earn our colors or, in other words, our special hunt outfits. We earn our colors by participating in the hunt; plus giving teas and donations for the daily care and exercising of the hounds. It takes about $345 a year to maintain one hound: kennels, food, veterinary, shots, and traveling to other hunts. We currently support 20 hounds and their litters.

Official hunt clothing consists of a bottle green hand-tailored jacket with a lemon yellow velvet collar. The brass buttons are engraved with the Spring Creek Basset Hunt insignia. The coat is worn with a cream-colored ascot and the same color of britches. Boots and a black velvet hat complete the colors. During the formal hunt ball, a number of men sport tailcoats in the same hunt colors. Women wear either a long gown or appropriate ballroom attire.

The Spring Creek Basset Hunt originated in 1968. Basseting endures thanks to certain gentry and other assorted eccentrics. The sport and rituals are exciting. To stay with basseting, however, you definitely have to be a little quirky.

TALLYHO!

☙

Jane F. Jackson treaded the upheaval of several careers and relationships; currently, she savors the peace of retirement. She lives in Chicago and writes short stories, dances the Argentine Tango, hunts with the Spring Creek Basset Hounds, and boats the waterways of Illinois.

ɞ Inez Boler

THE YEAR HAS GROWN OLD

The year has grown old. The grey November days are short and sunless. From my kitchen window, I watch the red light at dawn creeping upward in the east, shoving aside the dark edge of night. The city sleeps. It is the quiet hour with only the sound of the perking pot breaking the silence, filling the room with the aroma that promises a fresh cup of coffee to start my day. With the Thanksgiving holiday over, Christmas looms on the horizon. Already colored lights and sparkling tinsel are beginning to appear in the windows of my neighborhood. Soon, I must look for the cluster of sequined acorns tied together in a wreath with red and green ribbons that decorates my window each year. The sequins have lost some luster and the ribbons are frayed, but this is my 77th Christmas. The excitement of the holiday does not have the intensity of first Christmases.

Vagueness clouds my first memory of Christmas. I must have been less than four years old, because I was still the only child in the household. My parents, like most first-time parents, were certain that they had created an exceptional child which, with proper rearing, would become a perfect adult. Even at less-than-four, I did not accept this premise enthusiastically, which probably accounts for my skepticism when my mother told me about this man in a red suit trimmed with fur, who would stuff my stocking with toys if my behavior was impeccable. According to her, this weird man in the red suit would come sliding down the chimney with a bagful of goodies.

Perhaps the basis of my doubt was the fact we did not have a fireplace. Our small home was heated by a pot-bellied stove, with large, black pipes that entered the wall and extended to the rooftop, where it ended as a brick chimney. Throughout the winter, this stove was filled with flaming chunks of coal emitting puffs of smoke which billowed out of the chimney. The idea that anyone would slide down through that mess raised a lot of questions. How did he get on the roof? How could reindeer fly if they didn't have wings? Could Santa Claus breathe smoke? Why didn't he burn up in the fire? How could he open the stove door from the inside? Why didn't he just come through the front door? Or the back door? Or the window? Well, couldn't we just leave the key in the door? Did I mention that my mother was a patient woman?

Nevertheless, when Christmas Eve arrived, I still had no intention of doing anything so ridiculous as hanging up a stocking. But my mother was also a persuasive woman, and I did really want to please her, even to the extent of honoring her radical ideas. I hung up a long, white-ribbed cotton stocking, probably on the top of the varnished wainscoting that decorated the lower half of the room.

The physical details are only hazy memories, but the intense emotional shock that I felt when I saw the gifts in my stocking the next morning remains. I became an instant believer in fairy tales, miracles, fantasies and all my mother's wild stories.

Unfortunately, it was not in my nature to accept this new concept unconditionally. I had to probe the depths. The philosophical purpose of Christmas had eluded me, but I quickly grasped its beneficial possibilities. It occurred to me that maybe this strange Mr. Santa Claus could be lured into giving gifts any time one hung up a stocking; so the next night, I repeated the procedure.

Morning came, I awoke with anticipation and hurried down the stairs before my parents were up. Mr. Claus had indeed visited our house again, but to my total humiliation, instead of gifts he had put a dry bread crust in my stocking. Apparently, he had been watching and had noticed that I always refused my mother's requests to eat the crusts as well as the bread. My respect for Mr. Claus increased.

Then, lest my mother discover this reprimand by Santa Claus, I hid the bread crusts under the china closet that held my mother's favorite dishes. When she first began to question me about what Santa Claus had put in my stocking, I replied, "Nothing." I stuck with this answer for quite some time, but as I told you my mother was a very patient and persuasive woman. Eventually, her persistence succeeded, and I told her the truth, including the current location of the bread crust.

Many Christmases have come and gone and been forgotten. This one remains in my memory, perhaps because I learned two important facts that Christmas: one, that Santa Claus was smarter than I was and, two, that my mother was almost as smart as Santa Claus.

I WRITE A LETTER

I am forgetting words. In the middle of a conversation, a word that once came so easily will suddenly be lost in the files of my mind and I pause, struggling to find a substitute. Words are so important. Words can create fear. Words can create joy. Words can be strung like beads into phrases that glitter like a necklace. Words can be woven like thread into dark emotions or happy emotions. And now I am forgetting words.

It was the letters brought by the mailman that first piqued my interest in words. My mother would open the envelopes and become absorbed with the ink scratches on the sheets of paper found inside. Sometimes they made her sad, other times they made her smile. When my father came home from a place called work, she shared the letters with him and if I let them know that I was feeling left out, I was allowed to "read" the letters too.

Diligently, I studied every variation in those letters, every nuance that might reveal the secret of their power to move emotions. I observed that sometimes the scribbles were round shapes that dropped below the line, while others rose above the line. Some were crossed with a bar, and others had dots above them. There were also dots on the lines and white spaces between the scribbles. Some scribbles were short and some were very long. Armed with all this information, I felt confident that I could now write a letter. I explained my intention to my mother who promptly provided me with pencil and paper. Using the seat of a kitchen chair as a desktop, I stood beside it writing many pages following carefully the aforementioned rules. After finishing, I looked over the pages with great pride . . . and wondered what I had written. Since my mother was in the process of preparing the evening meal, she did not have time to tell me, but promised that, "When daddy comes home, he will read it to you."

I waited. When he had settled down in the rocking chair with the homemade pillows, when he had packed tobacco into the bowl of his pipe, lit it with a large wooden match and pulled heavily until the tobacco caught the flame, I brought the letter to him.

"I wrote this today," I said.

"Hmm!" he said, looking it over. "Very good!"

"Will you read it, daddy?" I asked, climbing on to his lap.

As he read each page, I discovered that I had written a fabulous story which even included some words that I didn't know I knew. When he had finished the story, I gazed at him in spellbound awe.

"Did I really write all that?" I asked.

"I only read what was on the pages," he assured me.

Although the story has been forgotten, disintegrated to dust like the paper it was (allegedly) written on, the magical belief that I had written it remains like a bright light in my memory. And it had been so easy. All I had to do was cross my t's, dot my i's and remember my p's and q's.

HARD ROCK BEAT

I have a hammer in my hand. Walking quietly, I enter the apartment and hit the new tenant exactly in the center of her skull. I pound the skull over and over and over again. The blows are intensely rhythmical . . . boom, boom, boom. The hammer does not stop the beat. The hard metal rock beat that severs the subconscious from the conscious, that tears the body from the soul, that destroys the communication with the collective unconscious. It is a beat that was born in hell.

I open my eyes and look at the clock: 2:30 A.M. I must have dozed off. The leaves on my plants seem to be trembling in the half light from the street lamp shining through the window. My cactus, which started blooming on Thanksgiving Day and which was not to be moved lest its blossoms fall, is now blossomless. The tape that I had put on the recorder because it was supposed to neutralize noises has stopped, probably aware that its effort was futile. Nothing can overcome the party music emanating from the apartment two floors beneath ours.

Walking to the kitchen, I pour a cup of hot tea from the glass pot sitting on the pilot light of the gas stove. I swallow an insomnia pill. I stare out the window. The night is too long. Tomorrow, I had planned to finish writing a journal piece for a class I take. Now I know that sleep deprivation will make that impossible. I must live the life style of the new tenants living in the apartment two floors below us.

Through the window, I stare at the snow-covered roots of the stark trees. The winter is too long. I have been old for a long time, too long. When the CTA informed me that my ID card would have to be renewed, I assumed that they knew some secret that I didn't know. Perhaps, having reached the age of 65, the process would be reversed and we would grow younger. Maybe there was some new youth renewal potion about to be released on the market.

The walls are still vibrating with the loud bass of the hard rock beat. I turn from the window, glance thoughtfully at the long sharp knife that I left on the kitchen table when I went to bed at ten o'clock. I go to the living room and lie down on the sofa. I close my eyes . . .

With knife in hand, I sneak quietly into the apartment of the new tenant . . .

༄

Inez Boler is mild mannered in speech and demeanor but her writing takes her from childlike whimsy to "mad enough to kill." Humor lurks behind all of it.

ᑲᓗ **Marta Melcher**

ONE FOR ME AND THE REST FOR YOU

When I was at Pipers Alley Theater Building today, I passed a checkroom with a young girl standing there waiting for customers with their hats and coats. It took me back forty years.

We were newcomers and had scraped money together to start our life in the U.S.A. Once in a while I had a chance to work in the checkroom of a Hyde Park hotel for occasions such as parties, weddings, etc. I was always the only person in the checkroom. The manager told me that all tips go to the hotel and I get 75 cents an hour.

One day, a lady who seemed to know her way around stopped by and told me, "When no one is around, put a few dollars in your coat pocket; the hotel will still get enough. No one should be made to work for 75 cents an hour." I followed her advice and had usually $3 or $4 on top of my 75 cents an hour. It depended upon the generosity of the customers.

One evening I was called to come to work because the Knights of Columbus had a major happening with a dinner and speakers—the works. One of the larger, upstairs banquet rooms was used for the occasion. The checkroom was not just a little hole in the wall with a cigar box for money. It was a real checkroom with a long counter separating it from the hallway. There were slots in the top of the counter into which patrons dropped the tip. The money fell into a drawerbox with a padlock on it. Well, I thought, no extra few dollars tonight.

Suddenly, I heard a friendly greeting and looked up. It was one of the pharmacists of the Walgreen's where I bought toothpaste and stuff. He told his Knights of Columbus friends that I was one of his customers and encouraged them to give me a big tip when they picked up their coats and hats. While I was very polite and friendly, my heart sank lower than the basement of the hotel. I think it went all the way to China. I left it there for a while, because then I had to rearrange the marbles in my head. When no one was around, I tried to pull out the drawerbox. That worked, but there was the padlock. I found a clean handkerchief in my purse and laid it across the slot in the drawerbox. The money would fall through the countertop slot and land on the handkerchief. As people never go home all at the same time, I was able to empty the handkerchief every so often, putting most of the money into the drawerbox and some aside for myself. It was a successful evening; I took home about $40.

Whenever I am downtown for the Columbus Day parade and the Knights of Columbus come marching along, I salute them in my mind and say, "Thanks, fellows, for buying such nice shoes and socks for my boys."

A LITTLE RED WAGON

When World War II was over and the dust had settled a little, some of the married American soldiers had their wives and children brought over the ocean to live in Germany while the soldier husbands were stationed there. As my hometown borders on what was then called Rhein-Main Air Base, I sometimes passed American women with their children on the street. Some of them pulled a most adorable little red wagon in which the children were sitting.

Right then and there, I made up my mind that I should buy a little red wagon like that when I got to Chicago. We finally got our travel papers and arrived in Chicago January 29, 1952. My husband's parents lived at 78th and Cornell Avenue. We stayed with them until we found our own apartment. Grandma Melcher, my husband's mother, did her grocery shopping at a Hi-Low store at 76th and Stoney Island. She took me along to show me all the tricks of supermarket trading. Later I went by myself, usually after returning from a walk with our boys.

As spring came, joy of all joys, the Hi-Low store displayed little red wagons all along their big windows. They called them Hi-Low Flyers and the price was $5.99. That evening after I first saw them, I told my husband all about my plan to buy such a vehicle. I convinced him that we could afford to buy one for Easter and fill it with Easter eggs.

That is how the Easter Bunny found us in Chicago and brought us a little red wagon with eggs and two chocolate bunnies. We enjoyed that wagon very much. We took it to the park and pulled our groceries home with it. We had made our first big step toward becoming Americans.

Twenty-two years later, when my first grandchild, Karla Melcher, was born, I went to Marshall Field's and bought her a beautiful red wagon with a wood railing all around. It cost about 10 times the price of that first red wagon, and I really thought I had arrived. I got what I came to America for. Please forgive me for ending the sentence with a preposition, but I wanted to say it in real American. Yes, I got what I came for and I could afford it, thanks to my simple taste and realistic aspirations.

"MIST"

"The next play we read in our group will be *Mutter Courage* by Berthold Brecht. The play is set in the 17th century and the 'Thirty Years'—so called religious—War." Reading the play at home and thinking about the historical setting, I was reminded of an incident at Chicago Vocational School in the Americanization class.

It was in fall 1952, my English teacher—sorry, I forgot her name—was talking about the Pilgrims on the shores of this continent in 1620. She told me that they were English people who had fled from religious persecution. As she was always trying to encourage her pupils to speak, formulate sentences, and use the words they had learned, she asked about historical happenings of the 17th century in the different countries from which all of us came. When the entire class was sitting in silence, I thought someone has to start, and I raised my hand. I stuttered along using the few words I knew. In Germany at that time was also an upheaval over religion. It was the Thirty Years War from 1618-1648. I tried to tell how it started. It was in Prague, the Protestant Bohemian nobles had a meeting in the castle and some representatives of the Catholic German Emperor (House of Hapsburg) came also to that meeting. Tempers flared and two of the emperor's sons were thrown out of the window. I tried to tell the teacher and the class that the two men really did not get hurt because they fell on . . .? Well, I did not know the word for the stuff on which they fell. I turned and asked a German fellow who sat behind me if he knew the English word for "mist." He did not know it either, but suggested to call it "garbage of the animals." Good idea, and I passed it on to the class and the teacher. Then the teacher wrote on the blackboard, "manure, muck, animal dung."

I still think it was an important lesson for newcomers in a world city with neighborhoods where people have gardens and where a terrific institution, the Lincoln Park Zoo, provides for people to enjoy and smell manure.

☙

Marta Melcher writes (and speaks) English with a German inflection, but thinks like the great American she is. She says, "It was a pleasure to discover America in 1952, part of which was learning a second language. Being a member of the Journal Writers at Renaissance Court is one of the rewards of my labor."

❧ Frances J. Markwardt

BABY

She sold the baby formula for drugs
and the baby died.
A tiny little piece of flesh
that must have cried in rage
and kicked its little legs
as hunger gnawed its bowels.
She missed the contented nuzzling sounds
of her baby suckling,
happy waving arms with joy,
a brief and precious smile,
a little human being
who needed her.
All gone.

TO CLIMB A LADDER

My friend who is 65 years old
fell off a ladder.
Stupid foolish thing to do we said
to climb a ladder
when you are 65 years old.
But he said if he had climbed

Frances J. Markwardt

the ladder and come down safely
we would all be saying
what a wonderful thing he did
to climb a ladder
when he's 65 years old.

He's right, we know.
Would we say to somebody who was 45 or 50
What a stupid thing to climb a ladder
or what a wonderful thing to climb a ladder?
At 45 or 50 it's just to climb a ladder
and if you fall
you fell off a ladder at 45 or 50.

☙

Frances Markwardt is sixty-six years old and just started writing poetry. "I don't know how my poems rate, but if I had known how much fun I'd have writing them I'd have started a long time ago."

❦ RAYMOND WENTWORTH

EARLY TIMES

Memory gets a little tricky these days. Where was I going to go when I got up from my chair? What's the adjective I thought was right there on my tongue? When did I forget my best friend's first name? Who's the composer of one of my favorite pieces of music, the one that's being played on WFMT right now?

I've heard it said, jokingly, that the worst time is when you are interrupted on a stairway, then can't remember whether you were going up or going down. My response is that you were most likely going to whichever floor has the bathroom.

Ah, but looking back to earlier days shows a clearer view. I have several early memories that are essentially undated, but there is one clear memory from the time I was two—and just barely that—and one I know dates back to when I was three. Would you believe food is a central element in both of them?

My father was what was known as a "good provider," even though he was a schoolteacher. For one thing, he always, for as long as I can remember, maintained a garden and produced lots of fresh fruits and vegetables for the family. For another, he always taught, for extra money, in the summer school the local YMCA held for those students who couldn't "hack it" during the school year, or who wanted to get ahead on required subjects so they could take electives dear to their hearts in the regular school term.

But when late August came around, the family always headed for the Atlantic Ocean beaches for a one- or two-week holiday at a "tourist court," a semicircle of small, detached cabins that served roughly the same purpose motels do today. Some summers we went to Cape Cod, and some we went to the Maine coast, where the weather was likely to be colder and the beaches were likely to have a larger stone or pebble content.

The summer I turned two was one of the years we went to Maine. It was a cold year, and the week we spent there was grey and foggy, and all of us were rather miserable by the end of our stay. I remember one morning, when I was really cold, we went to the nearby coffee shop and had breakfast. I sat between my two parents, being warmed by their proximity on either side, and ate hot oatmeal. What a comfortable experience!

Another time—I know that I was three because I've had occasion to tell the story many times since—I was in the little backyard on a warm spring day, and my mother decided to feed me outside. Through the back door she handed me a bowl of bread and milk, telling me she knew I would like it. I did. I sat down on the back steps and really enjoyed the treat. Afterward, I lay down on my back in the grass and looked up at the beautiful, blue sky, watching the fleecy clouds form magical shapes.

I was a little older, probably five or six, when the jelly roll incident took place. My brother, then 13 or 14, had added several inches to his height and an octave to the lower end of his voice range at the onset of puberty, and his appetite kept up with his stature. Breakfast for him might consist of a box of cereal and a quart of milk. He also was a lean, energetic type, and it was during that period that my parents bought 40 acres of field and woodlot in East Princeton, 13 miles from our house, using as an excuse John's need to have a place to burn off excess energy. Actually, though, what attracted my father probably was the chance to put in a really serious garden, which soon was producing so much food that I peddled it among our neighbors. The woods yielded firewood that kept us warm during the spring and summer—in cold weather we burned coke.

In any case, one night John, as usual, finished supper long before the rest of us, and a jelly roll was put in front of him. Slice after slice went into his mouth. I am told that my face fell when the last piece disappeared, and when my father saw I had given up any hope of having dessert, he quickly went out to the kitchen to get the *other* jelly roll, the one intended for the rest of the family.

MEET MY PARENTS

My mother, Willa Wentworth, was at an extreme disadvantage during my early childhood. Her pregnancy with me had left her with a persistent kidney infection (this in the days before antibiotics, and even before sulfa drugs) and she had to spend a great deal of her time flat on her back in bed. She did prepare my lunch and dinner for the family, but grocery shopping, floor washing, laundry and other chores fell to my father. Willa did spend a great deal of time with her younger son (who was me), and I have wonderful memories of her teaching me such things as the names of the colors, and how to make a pie crust (the scraps of dough were delicious, even raw, but especially when sprinkled with sugar and cinnamon and baked for a while).

By the time I was in school, however, the infection seemed to have cleared up, and Willa was able to take on an active role in the household and in the community. She and Everett both were ARP (Air Raid Precaution) precinct wardens; she specialized in watch and first-aid duties, and he in fire fighting preparations. Willa also served several years as precinct captain for the local American Red Cross fund drive. She often would make use of my legs to deliver collected funds to the ward captain, one Mrs. Hoyt. Funny how these names stick in the mind. I even remember the name of the fund drive chairman for many years for the entire city—Wat Tyler Cluverius. But then, who could forget a name like that?

My father, Everett Wentworth, served for many years as an officer of the Worcester County Education Association and was treasurer of a local Boy Scout troop. He worked hard at his job and had the respect of all the faculty at Grafton Street Junior High School, and the affectionate (usually!) respect of the students. Unless he had hall or cafeteria duty, he always ate lunch at his desk with students surrounding him — not necessarily his own — asking questions or for help in working out their problems on the board.

As I rode to school with him during my seventh, eighth, and ninth grade years, I can vouch for the fact that he always was in the classroom very early and washed his own blackboards before he was ready for the students who came in early for extra help. Meanwhile, I would read the comics in the Worcester *Telegram* and the Boston *Post,* which my father always would buy on the way to school.

The extra time I had to spend in school as a result of my father's love of teaching didn't gall me too much. I really enjoyed the rides with him and the chance to talk with him. I think he enjoyed the rides for the same reason.

Everett Lawrence Wentworth and Willa Page Wentworth both were Vermonters of old New England stock, my mother having been raised in the northern part and my father in the southern part of the Green Mountain State. Willa had graduated from [Peter Bent] Brigham Academy at the age of 15, and Everett, whose home was in East Dover, a hamlet without a high school, had made his way through Brattleboro High School by working and living in a plant nursery.

I think if my father had had his real druthers, he would have been a farmer. Instead, he established a fine academic record at what was to become the University of Massachusetts at Amherst, and immediately became the principal (and an athletic coach) of a small-town high school. Subsequently, he would take similar positions in increasingly larger high schools, until he decided to go back to the relatively less stressful position of junior high school mathematics teacher. The early onset of angina had been a warning.

Willa, meanwhile, had started teaching (a few days before her 16th birthday; it wasn't really legal) in a two-room schoolhouse in the north of the state. Later, she took two years off and went through North Adams (Massachusetts) Normal School, then she went back to teaching, stopping only when mothering demands made it necessary.

The two of them met one summer when they were employed at neighboring resorts on Lake Champlain. The story is that my father and a couple of the other hired hands amused themselves one sunny afternoon by turning a bureau mirror into a heliograph, and shining sunlight into the windows of the waitresses' rooms in the neighboring resort. That got the ladies' attention.

The First World War saw my father, as an army corporal, being gassed at Verdun. Convalescence was long, and the psychological effects lingered; Willa said that for a long time afterward, if a Klaxon horn sounded from a passing car during the night, Everett would wake up screaming and dive under the bed, searching for his gas mask.

Other things also caused Everett, a "high strung" individual, to lose sleep. Dearly as he loved the game of chess, he had to give up playing it, because he couldn't stop replaying a game in his mind all through the night, leaving him hardly fit for teaching in the morning. He took up the game again, and then in a modest way, only after he was 50 when I, as a choirboy of 10 with choir pay in my pocket, found a sort of chess set at the downtown Woolworth's and brought it home, expecting my father to teach me how to play.

That set, as I remember, was an improvisation, like many of the toys available during those World War II years. It was entirely of cardboard: a printed chess/checker board, and a card full of punch-out circles printed with the symbols of chess pieces on one side, red or black, and solid colors (for checkers) on the other. They weren't very elegant, but they got the job done. I remember my delight when, about the fourth time we played, I caught my father in a "fool's mate," winning the game. It was a long time before I won another game, and I sweated for every rare victory!

HOW GILBERT & SULLIVAN CHANGED MY LIFE

As a bright and relatively docile kindergarten student, not much was expected of me but to obey the teacher and do my best to please her. In spite of the fact both my parents were schoolteachers, I didn't know much about the importance of grades, or the matter of self-fulfilling expectations. I did know that, if a bad conduct report reached home, I would get my bottom smacked by my father. But I gave that little thought and I was content to ride along with the program. I was learning things, and that was fun.

My first report card day did come around, however, and I was the bearer of a mysterious envelope, carefully pinned to my shirt. My mother relieved me of the burden and opened the envelope. A strange look came over my mother's face; it wasn't disapproval, it was more of a questioning look. She gave me my lunch, and the afternoon went along in serene fashion.

But when the rest of the family came home, that report card was of even more interest to everyone than those my sister and brother had received. My sister, especially, was incredulous. The only unexpected mark was totally out of the blue; my mark in music was a C.

In those days, the schools of Worcester, Massachusetts, used an ABCD system, with D as failure, and C as average. In terms of percentages, for subjects where more precise values could be assigned, A represented an average grade of 90 to 100, B was 80-89, C was the broad span of 65-79, and D, a failing grade, was anything below 65.

Now, by the time I was five, I was regarded within my family as something of a *Wunderkind* in music. As an imitator of my older brother and sister, I was a singer before I was a talker, and I had a repertoire covering many of the folk tunes popularized by Burl Ives, and (reflecting my father's interests) many of the ballads of Blue Grass Roy, whose early morning radio program came on just after the Department of Agriculture extension reports, to which my father listened while he was preparing breakfast for the family.

It was the consensus (I had no opinion and was only peripherally interested in the discussion) that the kindergarten teacher probably had never actually heard me singing. My voice was not loud, as were the voices of some of my classmates; I sang with nicely placed head tones, and I was precisely on pitch, unlike many of my classmates.

My sister, Eleanor, took it upon herself to correct the situation. After supper, she took me over by the piano and taught me a song from her Gilbert & Sullivan collection. She then suggested that I ask my teacher the next day if she would like to hear me sing something I had just learned.

Of course, Miss Bacon would be very pleased to listen to me. I stood up straight, as I had been taught, put my hands by my side, and began:

"On a tree by a river, a little Tom-Tit
Sang Willow, tit-Willow, tit-Willow."

Miss Bacon was all ears. I continued until I had sung all three stanzas, never losing my audience, which also included most of my classmates.

Strange to say, for the rest of my school career I never received anything less than an A in music.

A TALE OF TWO TREES

It wouldn't be true to claim it was the prettiest Christmas tree in the world. It was only about two feet tall, and it stood in a plastic utility bucket filled with cat litter, in lieu of a stand. It was, in fact, rather scrawny, and it was far from symmetrical. Its plumage was sparse. Unquestionably, however, it was one of the two most memorable trees of our life together. It was a Christmas Eve purchase, and it cost fifty cents.

Dede was most gorgeously, extravagantly pregnant. "Something has come between us," was the joke when we were dancing, or just being affectionate. Sprout, as we called our joint creation at that point, was due in about three weeks, and as newlyweds still after 11 months, we were both excited by the prospect of parenthood. In our financial situation, however, we had to stretch our 1964 Christmas dollars as far as possible, and we wanted, for religious reasons, to delay the start of our Christmas until its Eve, and have a tree that would last into the Epiphany season.

We had been wed the previous January in All Saints Episcopal Cathedral, Milwaukee. As we were both faithful members of the choir, that group insisted on singing for us, and Dean Jacobs and Canon Heffner insisted on celebrating a Solemn High Mass. I asked the bishop (The Rt. Rev. Donald Hathaway Valentine Hallock—what a name!) if he wanted to make it a Pontifical Mass, but his answer revealed something important about the man: "I don't get a chance very often to sit in the congregation with my wife, and I'd like to do that, if you don't mind." Mind? I was flattered. His wife, Ruth, was a member of the Bible study group that had served as a springboard to courtship for Dede and me. My best man was my boss, Peter Day, the editor of *The Living Church* magazine, who soon was to become ecumenical officer for the Episcopal Church.

Love had come late and unexpectedly for me. I had fully resigned myself to living a single life and had never really dated, when along came this young lady who, two years earlier, had sung for a while in the cathedral choir before going away to join the Episcopal Franciscan Sisters on Long Island. Then one Sunday morning she was back, having been seen at the convent as a "problem like Maria," in *Sound of Music* terms. I dated her, intending, I said, to get her into circulation and very soon decided to take her out of circulation. The fact she was nine and a half years (I refuse to say ten years!) younger than I seemed to make no difference, but did make it desirable to waste no time in starting a family.

Almost immediately after our marriage it became obvious that two could not live on what the magazine could afford to pay me, so I had become a reporter-photographer for the *Beloit* [Wisconsin] *Daily News*.

Now the start of our family was less than a month away. During the week before Christmas, Dede's sinuses had started acting up and, with her doctor on vacation, she didn't dare risk harm to the baby-to-be by taking any medication beyond an occasional light dose of aspirin. She spent a great deal of time in bed and turned colored paper and aluminum foil into a wonderful collection of ornaments. When, on Christmas Eve, I came back with the little tree, we were able to put up a tribute to life and to the season that we both treasured.

Our very own "Maid Marian" was born in the early morning hours of January 16, 1965, so by the time the next

Christmas came around, we had not an 11-month-old marriage, as we had the year before, but an 11-month-old child.

Marian Willa Wentworth, by that age, was cooperative enough about meal times so that we were able to feed her early on Christmas Eve and settle her in for a nap, while I went to hunt down the wild Christmas tree. I found a suitably individualistic one, paid (I think) $1.50 for it, and brought it home, where Dede and I decorated it. By that time we had a string or two of colored lights, so we were able to make a thing of some beauty. Almost on cue, after we had finished and were sitting back, enjoying the scene, Marian woke up. Dede retrieved her from her crib and set her down in the hallway just outside the living room, then came to sit with me and watch Marian's all-fours entrance.

Marian started to come into the room, toward us, then stopped and took a look at the lighted tree. Her face clouded, and she turned around and retreated from the room for a minute or two, then ventured back into the room. For just a little, the unexpected Christmas tree had overwhelmed her. Very soon, however, Marian was getting as much enjoyment out of the tree as her parents were.

If then were now, we certainly would have had a video record of the scene. It has always seemed unfair that Marian, who entertained us so much with her hesitation entrance, couldn't have the benefit of seeing it herself.

༒

Ray Wentworth, a former newspaperman, finds his greatest joy in retirement in singing and writing music. Writing for the journal class not only sharpens his skills, he says, but gives him "an excuse for reliving wonderful times."

☙ Elaine M. Sheahan

NOSEDIVING THE CLIPPER

When I was in my late twenties, I worked with an elderly lady who was an acquaintance of a famous pilot named Pappy. I don't remember his last name. She told me many stories about Pappy. He was a real heroic pilot during World War I. He was also the first pilot to fly a mail plane across the United States. So, you see, Pappy wasn't exactly a youngster.

I was planning to drive from Chicago to Fremont, Michigan, to visit some friends and had to pass Muskegon, Michigan. Pappy owned a small airline and flying school located at the Muskegon Airport. Much to my delight, my friend Margaret made arrangements for me to meet him. She said he promised to take me up for a (as he put it) joy ride in one of his planes.

After driving for four hours, I arrived at the airport. It was the middle of July and a very hot and humid day. I was wearing terry cloth shorts and tee shirt. I had a pretty good figure in those days.

Inquiring at the airport for Pappy, I received a few curious stares, but thought nothing of them. I asked one fellow where I could find Pappy. He looked me over and said, "Well, well, well, Pappy's sure going to be surprised when he sees you!"

"Not really," I replied, "he's expecting me." The man shook his head, laughed, and walked away murmuring to himself.

Word spread fast, and soon I saw a little old man coming from one of the hangars. He was about five feet five, slightly built with a full head of white hair. He reminded me a little bit of Carl Sandburg, the poet, only quite a bit shorter. I was soon to learn he was no poet!

"Well I'll be damned," he blurted out. "I sure didn't expect to see such a purty young filly. When Margaret said you were friends, I thought you'd be a lot older."

He seemed to be full of pep for his age. While treating me to lunch at a diner across from the airport, he put me at ease as he told me of his many exploits and adventures.

"Now," he said, after we finished lunch, "let's go up and fly!" I had been looking forward to this for weeks, not only to the flight, but to the thrill of flying with such a famous pilot. He took me to a small blue and white Piper Cub that had two seats in the front and a third in the back.

"That's the rumble seat," he explained.

After he described the controls, we took off. Pretty soon we spotted the old Milwaukee Clipper ship cruising the harbor below. It went from Milwaukee, Wisconsin, to Muskegon, Michigan. I had been on the ship several times, and it was a thrill for me to see it from above.

Giving me a sly look and a grin, he said, "Would you like to get a real close look at it, Honey?"

"Sure," I said, wondering how close was close.

"Hang on, here we go!" He dived down on that ship so fast and so low I thought we were going to crash right down on the deck. My heart was pounding, my body tingled and I thought I would wet my pants. I lost my stomach up in the air somewhere. He turned the plane around and dived down again. We were so close I could see the passengers on the ship staring up in horror.

"Stop! Stop!" I screamed. But Pappy was having too much fun to stop. He seemed to be reliving his days as a fighter pilot. Finally, he took a deep breath and said,

"There, how's that? Didn't you get a thrill out of that?"

"No," I stammered, "I was too scared."

He apologized, and asked me if I'd like to take the controls and fly the plane. Even though my nerves were still a little jangled, I didn't want to miss the opportunity.

We went over the controls again. I learned how to turn right and left, how to go up and down, and soon I found myself actually flying. Oh, what a thrill! I was in seventh heaven. So much that when I heard a click I didn't pay much attention, although I did see Pappy do something on the panel.

"How'd you like another kind of thrill, Honey?"

"No thanks, Pappy, this is enough for me." I was afraid he was going to dive down again. But Pappy had other ideas. Suddenly I felt his hand on my knee; it crept higher and higher. Then his other hand reached over to grab and pull me closer. That old codger was trying to attack me!

As I fought him off, I kept saying, "Take the controls, we're going to crash!"

"Oh, no we ain't, Honey," he said with a sly grin, "I put her on automatic control. She's flying herself. Come on, come on to Pappy."

His hands were all over me, and I knew I had to do something quick. I grabbed his left hand and pulled the thumb back until I heard a crack. (I didn't take that self-defense class for nothing.)

"OW!" He let loose of me instantly, said a few curse words and took over the controls. We made a beautiful, and to me, a grateful landing.

Apparently his crew got wind of this little filly from the big city flying with Pappy. They all gathered around when we landed, asking how the flight went.

"Fine," I said with a grin. "Pappy is fantastic pilot." I didn't want to give him the satisfaction of panicking.

"What's wrong with your thumb, Pappy?" one of the crew asked.

"Oh, I just got it caught in the door," was his reply.

A few minutes later as I returned to my car, I turned around and looked back. There was Pappy surrounded by his crew. They were all laughing and looking back at me. Pappy held up his thumb in a salute. I don't know if he meant "all is fine" or "look what you did to me."

The following week, my friends in Fremont sent me a clipping from the Muskegon paper stating that Pappy was fined and given a reprimand for his antics over the Milwaukee Clipper.

STRANDED ON A COUNTRY ROAD

It was late one Sunday morning in October when my husband and I left the family summer home in Lac du Flambeau, Wisconsin. We were headed back to Chicago after two weeks of vacationing in the upper part of the state. Our old car started acting up south of Madison. Since we still had 150 miles more to go, my husband decided to leave the main highway and get away from the mad rush of traffic. In case our old "clunker" didn't make it, at least we'd be driving on local roads, close to towns where we could go if necessary.

Old Betsy gave her last gasp of breath between two small towns with populations of under 500. It wasn't that the car needed gas; we had filled her up a hundred miles north. No, the old Ford was just plain tired. Of course, this had to happen in the middle of nowhere.

My husband took out the big HELP sign we always carried in the trunk for such emergencies, and he placed it inside the rear window. Then he put up the hood and we waited to be rescued. He assured me there would be someone along the road any minute. Although it was only four o'clock in the afternoon, it had started to turn dark. Looking up at the sky we could see a storm brewing. Fortunately, we had managed to get the car over to the side of the road before she went completely dead. It was pretty muddy there, but I was told that we would be safer over on the side than on the road, where we might be hit by another car.

"Hit by another car?" I said, "are you kidding? I don't know what county road we're on, but I doubt if any living being has used it for days."

His reply was, "Oh, you're worrying for nothing. I grew up on a farm and I know the farmers use these roads all the time."

I zipped my lip.

Of course, it started to rain. My husband was afraid the rain would ruin the motor, so he proceeded to put the hood back down. We both thought it was one of those quick fall storms, but the rain kept coming down harder and harder.

We must have sat there well over an hour. To make matters worse, I saw lightning strike a tree near by. Between that and the booming of thunder, I was beginning to be a basket case. But my mate reassured me the safest place to be during a storm was in a car. He said the lightning couldn't harm us because we were protected by the rubber tires. I didn't agree with that, but I gave him my usual reply (under stress, this time), "Whatever you say, dear."

Suddenly we heard a roar. I thought it was a tornado, but my husband (who's always right) said it was an airplane. It kept coming closer and closer. Whatever it was, was heavy, because as it approached, I could feel the ground shake. Poor Betsy was rattling whatever was left of her shocks under the car. The lights were so bright that we were temporarily blinded.

I was so terrified, I could feel the perspiration running down my body. I looked at my husband for support, but his eyes were bulging out of his head and he just sat there with his hands gripping the steering wheel.

Something, or someone, came out of the vehicle in front of us. It tapped on the window on my side. Running my hand over the window to clear the condensation away, I almost fainted. We were surrounded by little green people. They couldn't have been more than four feet tall, and they had antennas sticking out from the top of their heads!

By that time the rain had stopped, but it was still very dark. The little green people crawled all over the top of the car, jumping down into the puddles on the side of the road and giggling as they splashed into the water.

Suddenly, we heard a whistle and a loud booming voice seemed to be reprimanding the little ones. They all scampered down, and then we saw him. He must have been seven feet tall, with long black hair and a beard. He had a toothless grin. Two teeth out in the front of his mouth made the other front teeth look like fangs! Of course, my imagination really ran wild. All I could think of was Dracula. The black hat, pants, and long coat only added to the illusion. He went to the driver's side of the car and signaled to Jack to roll down the window. My naive partner stupidly complied as I sat next to him trembling with fear. By that time I was sure we had been invaded by creatures from another planet and visualized us being zapped, car and all, into that big monstrous vehicle ahead.

Suddenly we heard that voice again, saying, "Hi there, folks. Got car trouble, huh? Sorry about the little ones here." Then to the little monsters, he said, "All right now, you've had your fun. You kids line up now, like I told ya."

They meekly complied, and with sheepish grins they said in unison, "We're sorry if we scared you." Then, giggling, they all blurted out, "Trick or treat!"

The big guy turned out to be a local farmer with a cub scout group returning from a Halloween party. He hitched up the monster (it was a tractor) and pulled us to his farmhouse, where we all sat around drinking hot chocolate and eating cookies while one of his sons fixed our car.

A SENIOR'S WEEKLY JOURNAL

The older I get, the more I forget
Important events of the day,
It's strange how fast, I remember the past
Life's really funny that way.
I remember Sunday, that was the one day
That sticks in the back of my mind,
We went out for brunch, or perhaps it was lunch,
Whatever it was, we dined.
The service was buffet, I really must say,
I don't remember what I ate,
My platter was piled high from the salad to pie,
When I went home, I was ten pounds overweight.

But what I did Monday, that was the one day
I always seem to forget.
Did I write out those checks? Pay a few bills?
If not, then I think I'm in debt.
It was Tuesday, I think, when I flooded the sink,
The water flowed all over the floor,
My better half was mad, but I told him Ye Gad,
That's what plumbers are for.

Wednesday was an education, I got a citation
From the police for driving too slow,
I said I wasn't drinking, but only thinking,
Because I forgot where I was trying to go.
Thursday was a mess, I must confess,

Elaine M. Sheahan

It rained cats and dogs for hours,
So when did I find I was out of my mind?
When I was outside, watering the flowers.

I went to the grocer's on Friday
(It certainly wasn't my day)
My mind was pretty unstable,
After going through my purse
I started to curse,
I left my list on the dining room table.
Saturday was great, me and my mate
Went out for an elegant dinner
The service was divine, so was the wine,
But my hangover sure was a winner.

Journal writing is fun, and when this one is done,
Maybe I'll have someone bind it
Then I'll tuck it away for another day,
I just hope I'll know where to find it.
Modern medicine is wonderful I know
They have pills for the "runs"
And pills to make you go,
But I sure hope someday they'll find
Pills to help me find it,
When I lose my mind.

༄

Elaine M. Sheahan hears the rhymes and sees stories all around as she and her husband go about Chicago as performing artists in retirement venues. She keeps her journal filled with her observations.

ℰℐ **ELEANOR BALABAN-PERRY**

I COME OUT OF THE CLOSET

There's a standing adage—a compensation for aging—in my family that says "at this age you don't have to build character." I can say something off-color or do something that reveals a tinge of larceny in my soul, like never pay a bill until billed and should there be an error in my favor, pay it as is. If I find something of obvious value, it is not necessary to seek out the loser. I can stretch the facts to white lie status and be a bit dishonest (oxymoronic though it is). All this fudging goes under the umbrella of "at my age you don't have to build character."

All right, I don't really condone the above. But if I should, why not? I should accept me, all of me, as I am. At my age I don't have to hide anything. My daughter will still love me. And my friends probably know my weaknesses by now but still stay around, maybe out of habit, or love, or respect or maybe just convenience.

The important thing is that they are still around. Now I can admit what perhaps they already know or suspect. I can come out of the closet. I can lift the subterfuge. I can say it like it is.

They have called me sleepyhead since I was a child, and now I can say why. Yet I don't have to defend myself, explain myself. I can just accept the sobriquet and not be ashamed because I am a narcoleptic.

Many people do not know what narcolepsy is. I didn't until I was fifty years of age and was having my medical case history taken because of a heavy bronchial cough. I mentioned that I fell asleep at the drop of a hat, eating, walking, in the middle of anything and everything. The doctor was very perceptive and ordered an encephalogram that revealed the brain formation of a narcoleptic. Here is the characteristic performance of a narcoleptic. I never know when I am going to fall asleep sitting up or lying down. I can be eating, enjoying good food, even the company, and off I go to dreamland. I can sleep for a few minutes and wake up totally refreshed as if I have had a long night's sleep. Or I can go to sleep in my bed and have startling, frightening nightmares. I awaken and I can't distinguish between reality and unreality. Did it happen? Was I dreaming? Hallucinating? Or am I losing my mind? Sometimes when I awaken, my mind is racing, but I can't move. My body is paralyzed, I'm a prisoner in my own body grappling with fear.

One day I was walking down Chicago's Michigan Avenue in the din of rush-hour traffic, arm in arm with my daughter. I fell asleep, but continued to walk; that's automatic behavior. I didn't return to consciousness until my daughter shook me shouting, "Mama, wake up." I rarely laugh heartily even when the jokes are good, be it the best from a stand-up comedian. I must not indulge in any strong emotion like deep anger. That throws me off balance and I fall.

Once I fell asleep at a board meeting. The chairman, who was the only person I was accountable to, liked to touch big boobs on little women like me. Early in our association, I had to make it quite clear that he would have to evaluate my worth to the firm versus his roving hands. At this meeting he made an issue of my dozing, suggesting that I stay home nights and get some sleep. He enjoyed speculating on what he thought were my extracurricular activities since my divorce. Of course, I was embarrassed; but better to be thought a "loose" woman than a disabled narcoleptic.

Now that I no longer have to work for a living, I do not have to cover up my disability. Aged and retired, I live without mate or boss to witness my uncontrollable dozing. My degree of awareness is not paramount to the dollar earned. I no longer have to kowtow for a kopeck.

I can come out of the closet and honestly admit to one and all that I am a narcoleptic.

Could I be building character?

What? At my age?

THE REST OF ME

Not until I was a senior in high school did I discover the rest of me.

It happened by coincidence. Business complications took my father and mother to Canada to live. It was decided that I remain in Chicago to finish my senior year at Senn high school. I went to live with my maternal grandparents who were Orthodox Jews. It was already quite a household when I moved into that six-room flat on Lawndale Avenue. There were seven of us: Grandma and Grandpa, their young son Irving, their daughter Ethel and her husband Lawrence, their baby Betty Joy and me. Three families under one roof.

The through flat had three small bedrooms, a large kitchen and an ample dining room used only for company and high holidays. Up front was a living room with two window-like openings and a doorway that led to a sunroom, the width of the building, that was laden with grandma's greenery. Aunt Ethel and her husband shared the bedroom off the kitchen with their child who was already outgrowing her crib. Grandma and Grandpa used the middle bedroom and I was given the master bedroom. It had been Irving's room and now, since I was the paying guest, he was relegated to a daybed in the sunroom. No wonder it was difficult for him to breathe among all of grandma's greenery.

Since Irving was only two years older than I, he seemed more like a surrogate brother than the uncle he actually was. He was a change-of-life child, evidence that Grandma considered *di shande,* her shame, since it flaunted to the world that she and Grandpa were still doing it.

A wonderful relationship developed between Irving and me that year. He introduced me to all of his boyfriends. For a fifteen-year-old girl to be thrust among so many potential boyfriends was a windfall of secret happiness. True, they were mostly impoverished Jewish intellectuals and musicians, but nevertheless potential dates for a high school senior. Once a month we would gather at the home of one of Irving's friends for an evening musical from a quintet of amateur classical musicians. Irving was practicing hard on his clarinet hoping one day to be asked to join the group.

Even though we were three distinct families, I don't recall any fights or dissension. Periodically, Grandma and Ethel raised their voices. Both of them must have felt great strain reconciling the conflicting needs of their husbands and children. How well the two women handled the situation. There they were two generations, a mother and a daughter: one a first-generation American, the other a Russian immigrant. One non religious, who in her first pregnancy, called the baby she was carrying "porkchop." Aunt Ethel herself told me how during her pregnancy she and Uncle Lawrence would steal out, after Grandma and Grandpa had gone to bed, to make a weekly visit to the American lunch counter on Kedzie Avenue for a juicy porkchop. She lost the little fellow, he was stillborn. No wonder she was overjoyed to carry through with Betty Joy, truly the joy of her life. She never put the child in her crib without first lullabying her to sleep in the wicker rocker in Grandma's sunroom.

Supper served in the kitchen at a round oak table showed the difference between the two families. Uncle Lawrence's place at the table was laid differently than anyone else's, having a cloth napkin, a plate and side dishes. He liked separation of his foods while the rest of us had one plate where everything mingled happily. His vegetable was put in a side dish and the dinner plate was reserved for his steak or chop. Our potted meat, boiled potato and overcooked vegetable were heaped on one plate. Betty Joy's highchair was next to her father. She was a growing child and Ethel insisted on following a diet set by the pediatrician. Grandma, even though she kept the kosher dietary laws, in her wisdom permitted Ethel to cook bacon on the stove but in a separate pan reserved for *treyf,* forbidden food. There was a place for Ethel but rarely occupied by her. She often skipped meals saying she was dieting. She did her munching off-hours. I can still see her standing in the kitchen in front of the silver painted radiator rubbing her behind against its warmth as she ate a piece of rye bread smeared with chicken fat and rubbed with garlic (garlic bread Yiddish style) and cracked into a crisp Macintosh apple.

My food was slightly different, too. I had a glass of milk even if we were eating meat. Again Grandma relaxed the dietary laws to accommodate a grandchild. She said it was all right for me to mix dairy foods with meat, that is *milchik* with *fleishik.* If she were to do it, she assured me, she would become violently ill to the point of vomiting. Psychologically sound. Her stomach would reject what her mind had been conditioned to consider unacceptable.

Grandma never sat down to eat until all of us had finished, the table cleared and the dishes dumped into the sink. She hovered over Irving and me. Most of the time the *alter,* the old one as Grandma called her husband, ate by himself. He never ate without putting his *yarmulke* on his head. His diet was mainly soup, meat and potatoes. He refused most vegetables and literally sneered at salad greens saying he was a man not a rabbit. He took a schnapps before his supper and ended his meal at the sink with a cube of sugar in his mouth dissolving it with a glass of water. That was his dessert.

Aunt Ethel carried the brunt of the housework including the backbreaking rub-by-hand laundry, her family's, grandma's and mine, too. She also did the grocery shopping from two separate lists and paid out of two separate purses. Aunt Ethel acted like a cantilever balancing both sides fairly of what could have been an intergenerational disaster.

Sunday was special. For one, I stopped going to Christian Science Sunday School. Mom agreed to that. There was no sense in rubbing Grandpa's nose in the fact that his grandchild was being brought up in Christian theology. In the morning Irving, his cheeks inflated, tooted on his clarinet with his foot tapping out the beat of *Scheherazade*. In the afternoon, all of us except Grandpa gathered in the living room before the carved walnut console to listen to the radio broadcast of the New York Philharmonic direct from Carnegie Hall. The concert over, Uncle Lawrence would make some anecdotal comment regarding the piece or the composer.

It was a fruitful senior year that taught me many things. The world of classical music was opened to me. I also found out how few real friends I had among my lake front school chums. Only one came to see me, taking the streetcar west to unfashionable Albany Park. Best of all I gained my Jewish heritage. I even learned to speak fractured Yiddish while Grandma improved her broken English.

☙

Eleanor Balaban-Perry, an early radio script writer, mail order entrepreneur, and creative advertising director, now revels in her fourth career as editor/writer.

❦ Julia C. Attwood

THE FEMINIST MOVEMENT AND ME

I do not believe my nieces would be proud of my "feminist" ways.

In college my English tutor suggested I write my senior dissertation on literature by women. I indicated a strong lack of interest, mumbling to myself that, if he wanted to know about it, he could read it. Instead I selected Browning's poem "Saul," a tragic recitation indeed. Shortly after this, I discovered Dorothy Sayers' "Are Women Human?" That is what I wanted to be, not categorized, just a human being.

My next encounter with feminist reactions occurred in the 1950s while I worked for the public relations division of Michigan Blue Cross-Blue Shield. Detroit had suffered through a particularly horrendous summer, speeding the company's installation of air conditioners. It was about to enter the budding computer world and the computers, though not the people, had to be protected against the heat. In anticipation of entering this new era, all executives were required to attend computer training. I duly reported this back-to-school movement in an article for the company's house organ. I mentioned the instructor and what she was presenting. When the article was edited by the executive director, he changed all references to "she" to "the instructor." Our Blue Cross executives could not admit that a "she" knew more than they did and had even taught them about computers, of all things. I remembered this instance in the late seventies when I was lecturing on HMOs (health maintenance organizations) to a group consisting of all men. Yes, there was some satisfaction.

After the Blue Cross experience, I did not think much about my feminist stance until the late 1960s or early 1970s when I was in Cleveland. Responding to increasing interest from and demand on the part of women to enter the work world, the city government encouraged supervisors to consider volunteer work when judging applications. I was indignant. I had started at the bottom; I resented the newcomers' desired shortcuts to the top. I even was against equal pay during the first year of work, feeling that women first should prove their seriousness about working.

Attitudes change, even mine. I was proud of my profession and my contributions to it. Nevertheless, in the 1970s I still felt more humor than indignation over feminist slights. One of my tasks at this time was to sign, on behalf of the U.S. government, contracts for loans for hospital construction. Usually the lawyer and I would travel to the site, and I would read while he hammered out the legal intricacies. When my turn came, I signed. One time the lawyer and I trotted out as usual, only to find that the hospital was turning the "signing" into a gala occasion. The hospital executives looked surprised when I arrived and quickly ushered me to a table of all women, their wives. Throughout the meal we discussed making strawberry jam and other things unfamiliar to me, the working woman. I didn't mind. I like to glimpse into other kinds of lives. At the end of the banquet the hospital administrator signed the loan contract with a flourish and trooped out to celebrate. Caught off guard, the government lawyer came over to me to see if I had signed it. "No," I replied.

"But then they don't have a loan," he said.

"I know," I commented as he took off after the executives. They returned, at least the financial officer did, not as sheepish as he should have been, but enough so to grumble a sort of apology.

Admittedly, I have viewed the feminist movement with a touch of humor. On the other hand, I appointed women to high positions within the organization.

OOPS! I'M GROUNDED

My colleague John frequently mentions flying to Washington, D. C., to go to an opera. I remembered that when I saw a notice of the Vermeer art exhibit at the National Gallery. Thinking about John's comments and wondering how I could celebrate this special birthday, I decided, "That's it." I would fly there for the weekend and indulge in art. It seemed so jazzy and modern. Armed with tickets and reservations, I was on my way.

Monday was a beautiful day. Walking from the hotel to the gallery was a treat. I marveled at the long line of ticket hopefuls, some having arrived as early as 2:00 a.m. For those of us with advance tickets there was no delay in entering the exhibit area and, with perseverance, I was able to see all the paintings. They were beautiful and engaging. I looked forward to seeing them again the next day, for I had ordered tickets for consecutive days on the theory of "what is good once is better the second time." In the meantime, I sought out the gallery's Monet paintings and some favorites that I visit whenever I go to the gallery. Then I decided to stroll back to the hotel leisurely and watch the Super Bowl.

That is when my agenda changed. I certainly was not thinking deep thoughts at the time. Momentarily I wondered about which side of the street to walk along and decided to let the traffic light make up my mind. I may well have been admiring the blue sky, for indeed it was a beautiful day. Then my thoughts were suddenly focused. Without warning I found myself sprawled on the pavement, conscious of the blood flowing closer and closer to my coat. I really did not want it to soak in because I had to wear it home. As seconds went by I realized I would be unable to get up and so only could lie and wait. Fortunately, a young couple with a three-year-old, tourists from West Virginia, came along the otherwise deserted street. Quickly sizing up the situation, she told him to go and call 911. The little boy seemed bemused, wondering about this body lying unnaturally on the pavement. To reassure him, I noted that his red pants matched his mommie's jacket.

Soon the guard from the Department of Education office building arrived and, soon after that, the summoned ambulance. My education in emergency service began. The technician kept talking, obviously trying to determine how badly my bruised and scraped head had been damaged. I cannot remember the siren blaring much, but I was very aware of the lack of springs and the freezing air coming in from somewhere. I asked where we were going and was told to the George Washington Medical Center, the same emergency room where President Reagan was taken when he was shot.

I was attended to immediately. The head passed the tests although they correctly forecast two black eyes and a welt on my forehead. My lip was split but teeth intact. The arm however was subjected to X-ray. I knew I was in trouble when someone said I was a real trooper. There and back here, people admired the distance between where the dominant bone was and should have been. Another small bone was shattered beyond the possibility of restoring. I was in trouble because of the bone. I became a favorite patient however after I mentioned having a Vermeer ticket for the next day. The nurse took it eagerly and gratefully, saying she could not use it because of her duty schedule, but assuring me that it would be used by some thankful member of the staff.

In my state of confusion and shock I was given the choice of having surgery done there or being bound up in a temporary cast so that it would be safe for me to fly home. I chose the latter and, with the help of a niece and nephew, boarded the plane for a draining flight home. Then I gave myself over to the various doctors, glad to be freed from making decisions.

CASTING IT ASIDE

Coming around the corner into the waiting room was the persistent buzzing sound of the saw. I hoped the surgeon had a steady hand because my turn was next. As I waited I said my final bargaining prayer, the kind familiar to all of us: "If only I can sign checks, if only I can sew, then . . ." I also looked down at my cumbersome, almost arm-length encasement and hoped that out of the cocoon-like cast would come a butterfly.

Soon it was time for me to move beyond the waiting room. I found not only my surgeon but also a discriminating saw. It understood the difference between cutting through fiber glass and skin. It simply would not hurt the latter. "Try explaining that to four-year-olds," said the doctor. "They know a saw when they see it; they hear the racket, but they cannot accept the idea of a programmed blade."

By the end of that conversation, the cast was sliced apart and ready to reveal its content. A butterfly did not emerge. Disclosed instead was a badly swollen limb, coated with discolored skin eager to be peeled off and a joint unwilling to budge even a fractional distance. Looking down at this thing in discouragement, concern, and dismay, I had to concede that my hopes and prayers for the immediate now were not to be realized.

I went back to the waiting room to learn the fate of a friend who had come limping in while I was shedding my cast. While waiting, I thought back to my childhood. One morning my mother asked me to go with her to the train station to meet my grandmother, who was returning from California where she had broken her leg. I was terrified, too terrified. to confess it. I did not know what a broken bone meant. Would my grandmother now be in two parts? What a relief to see her descend the stairs in one piece, swinging her plastered leg ahead and demonstrating her mastery of crutches. What reassurance to feel her pleasure upon seeing us and her home again. My world settled down as my terror receded.

My friend finally came out to where I was sitting. Fortunately, she only had a bad sprain although she would be dependent upon a canvas cast-like shoe for a month. We talked a few moments and then she went her way, and I stopped off for my first experience with physical therapy.

I am not yet reconciled to feeling worse now that the cast has been removed. In fact I wish it were on again so I could use it to bean persons who offer the encouragement that I do not want to hear. I do not want to hear that the pain will be worth it, I do not want a pep talk. I just want someone to say "I know and I'm sorry" when I blurt out "it hurts, it's hell." Next week I will be better able to rejoin the positive ranks, but not just yet.

இ

Julie C. Attwood says she was fortunate to have had a varied career in the Public Health Service where she developed and administered new programs. She is a Midwesterner at heart and is enjoying her retirement in Chicago.

ᘏ Jim Merrill

RED IS FOR DANGER!

The Higbee family covered wagon lumbered along the indistinct ruts leading westward toward rich farm lands, lands reported by those who managed to get letters back East. The family of six was determined to leave the rocky soil of Vermont. Of English descent, mother, father, two sons and two of three daughters were all fair complected with carrot-top hair of the tint attributed to Elizabeth I. The third daughter drew her appearance from other blood lines; she was near olive complected with straight black hair. It was those looks that saved her life.

Somewhere in eastern Ohio an Indian raiding party came upon the family. It was hopeless by numbers alone. This coupled with the fact that Indians literally detested redheads led to the resulting tragedy. All redheads were killed; mother and father scalped, the children swung by their heels so skulls crashed against trees. Phoebe Maria Higbee, age five, was spared by the raiding party and was incorporated into their lifestyle.

A few months later missionaries visited the Indians' camp site and discovered Phoebe Maria. When confronted, the Indians admitted that she was indeed a white girl and surrendered her. These kind people then raised her from that time forward.

In the 1920s a patriotically, socially conscious relative aspired to join the DAR (Daughters of the American Revolution).

Anyone who has seen painter Grant Wood's "Daughters of the DAR" or his more famous "American Gothic" (a farmer with pitchfork and his wife in front of an Iowa Gothic church) knows about the DAR's then repute. The first painting depicted three acerbic ladies holding teacups. It was they who refused Marian Anderson, because of her color, the right to perform at Constitution Hall, which caused First Lady Eleanor Roosevelt to resign as a DAR.

To the point: a determined research of all the documented ancestral facts had a distinct short circuit; there was a distressing gap from one certain generation to the next. After heroic efforts at research, the revealing, if tragic, reason was found for the gap. Phoebe had used the given name of the missionaries who had faithfully recorded details in their Bible. Now my aspiring relative had a direct line to Grandpa. who fought at the Battle of Bennington, validating her membership in the DAR.

GRANNY AND THE GOOSE

My great-great-grandmother, Phoebe Basset Higbee, was a town girl married to a prosperous farmer whose farm was nearly a day's buggy ride away from her home in Fargo, North Dakota, back in 1843.

The capability of baking bread was very much missing from the list of Phoebe's attributes and talents. It took an unexpected overnight trip to town by great-great-grandfather Higbee to offer the opportunity for practice. Phoebe mixed and kneaded, then put the dough on a pantry shelf to rise. It didn't. Next morning the recalcitrant lump remained unrisen.

Disgusted, she took the unwilling mass out behind the barn and pitched it. In a flash a resident gander dashed up and gulped an enormous portion of dough, a fatal portion, as it seemed. Almost immediately Mr. Gander found his craw

117

jammed with dough, resulting in noisy suffocation. In other words, he croaked!

Ms. Phoebe reacted promptly; there would be roast goose for dinner this night. She quickly wrung the gander's neck and went to fetch a hatchet to complete the job.

When she returned, Mr. Gander was complacently waddling around the farm yard, pecking at grain. She had wrung the dough down the craw, restoring air and life to that silly goose!

&

Jim Merrill, retired industrial advertising executive, enlisted at age 17 in Army Engineering from the University of Kansas. Toured Europe with General Patton (Combat Infantry, Purple Heart). Back to school for B.S. degree, Northwestern University on G. I. Bill.

℘ Joey Goldsmith

WHAT TIME IS IT, ANYWAY?

When I was growing up, we were taught that unless you were one half-hour early for an appointment, you were actually late! I have vivid memories of being at the airport two hours before departure, or standing on the appointed street corner way ahead of schedule, or meeting a train and having to kill a full hour while awaiting its arrival. Old habits die hard and to this day I will arrive at wherever I'm going way ahead of schedule and silently curse whomever it is that is "late." When I add this disgusting habit to forgetting to call the airline in advance for arrival times, I've only myself to blame. When I get to O'Hare and need to make the time go faster, I have to resort to sitting and eating a hot dog that costs $7.

You'd think I would have learned a lesson. When I was invited to a 7:00 p.m. party recently, I had the audacity to show up at 7:00! The host and hostess were barely out of the shower when I rang their doorbell. I was told to make myself at home and they would be with me shortly. After reading *War and Peace* from cover to cover in their library, I was ecstatic to have some other guests arrive and make me feel less idiotic.

Along with this goofy habit is my other idiosyncrasy of going to bed very early. Many is the evening that I've been awakened by the phone at the ungodly hour of 9:30 p.m. and feigned being alert.

Do you think it's possible that an old dog can learn new tricks?

WILL WONDERS NEVER CEASE?

I'm known as a traveling grandmother. That could be a very positive statement, but when you come right down to it, what else can you do when all the grandchildren live elsewhere?

The most recent visit was in the early part of February. Before I left for Washington, D. C., my daughter said on the phone, "On Friday night we will attend the awards dinner." In Amy's mind, this was synonymous with the Academy Awards or the Nobel Peace Prize because both of her sons (ages 11 and 8) were to receive special recognition as Cub Scouts. The preparation for this gala event was incredible. There was a great to-do over getting the boys' uniforms assembled, their faces washed, and their hair combed. Finally, it was time to depart, with my daughter's potluck contribution in hand.

The atmosphere was in a feverish pitch as we approached the school, and once the boys found their respective friends, we adults were all but forgotten. After a ceremony or two, the various awards were announced and this grandmother swelled with pride as the badges were dispersed to my grandsons. (My next thought was that Amy would be sewing badges on uniforms for the next week!)

After dinner, we were directed to the gym, where an ex-Harlem Globetrotter by the name of Spinney Johnson was going to entertain a gym full of boys, their respective parents, and me, the lone grandmother.

After a few episodes of calling up a few boys at a time to engage them in various and sundry basketball "tricks,"

Joey Goldsmith

Spinney walked over to me and said, "Come on up here, grandma. Are you married? No? Well, will you marry me?"

When I answered in the affirmative, we all but set the date before we got to the center of the gym for the trick he had contrived for the two of us. Spinney was one of the few short basketball players I had ever seen, so I all but towered over him. And this was the trick: while spinning the basketball madly on his finger, he transferred it to a pencil on which a spoon was attached. He then handed this goofy ball, pencil and spoon to me, while putting a dish of Cheerios cereal in my other hand. My mission? To feed Spinney the Cheerios while the ball continued to spin! I must have done something right because there was raucous applause while I returned to my seat feeling like the world's biggest idiot. Unbeknownst to me, my daughter took pictures! On the way home, my eight-year-old grandson asked me if I was really going to marry Spinney!

THE GRASS IS ALWAYS GREENER

Have you ever wished your eyes were blue
When plain brown eyes were born to you?

Or yearned for straight hair, like every girl
Instead of fighting with every curl?

Or what about a sexy voice
Do we ever really have a choice?

D'ya ever wish with all your heart
That you could paint great works of art?

Or long to sing a song on key
When musical you'll never be?

Ever longed for tapered nails
When typing well just always fails?

Ever wish that you could be
A TV personality?

Or wish that you were tall and trim
Like gals that work out at the gym?

Have suburbs been your special dream
When city life just makes you scream?

Ever wished you were one of those
Who always managed perfect prose?

The list goes on and I can see
I rather like just being me.

∞

Joey Goldsmith, who has been writing verse all her adult life, was a writer/producer of amateur theatricals. Now she is active in NUILR (Northwestern University Institute for Learning in Retirement), Y-Me, and still has time for her four grandchildren.

☙ Roselyn K. Wozniak

ACTION NEAR THE MAILBOX

I had taken the train home from school. I spotted my friend Vicki going to the mailbox, so I walked with her. She mailed her letters and we started back across 99th Street. Now, crossing 99th Street in Chicago is an art form in itself. When the train has gone through, there are cars all over the place. Vicki and I were crossing in our usual manner. A man in a car didn't like our style. He expressed his displeasure by hurling an epithet at me.

I took exception to his remark and, being more mischievous than malicious, I plucked off his sunglasses. As Vicki and I were continuing on home, I was grabbed and told I was under arrest! As it happened Mr. Sunglasses was Mr. Policeman, and I was indeed and in fact arrested.

So there we were, the cop, Vicki, and I at the train station. He was holding my hand in a definitely nonromantic way. I was looking at him with a mixture of anger and fear. I was picked up in a squad car and taken to our local police station, which is old and small. Because it doesn't have a lockup (cells), offenders are transported by paddy wagon elsewhere. I had to be sent in a separate one, because the guys were afraid of me.

At the lockup my fellow criminals and I were standing in a group waiting to be let in. I was the prettiest woman in the group. By this time my sense of humor had returned, and I kept having to suppress a giggle. We were waiting to be let "in."

There were two women guards in the women's cells, one was doing counted cross-stitch, the other was knitting. It was knitting's turn. She asked me to remove anything loose from my head to my toes, fingerprinted me, and took my picture, front and side. After unrolling some toilet paper for me, she escorted me to my cell.

My place of confinement was clean and quite roomy for one person. A friend of mine, who gets arrested on a regular basis, gave this lockup good grades. On one wall there was a bench big enough to lie on. There was a combination all-in-one-piece, stainless-steel toilet, washbowl and drinking fountain. The men were on the other side of the wall. One man would periodically rattle the bars quite loudly. I sat on the bench and wished that I had a harmonica that I could play mournfully, that is if I could play a harmonica. I thought about prison jokes and prison movies. Where was my tin cup to run along the bars and were they going to feed me? The woman next door said that she could kill for a cigarette. Just then the man did the bar-rattle thing again. I remarked that he maybe wanted one, too. We had a good laugh.

My prints cleared, and I posted bond. I was in the lobby, putting my shoelaces back in my shoes and waiting for my husband to take me home.

Huey

I was 16. Felix was still working for my dad. He would have a day off during the week. Dad would do Felix's job in addition to the baking that day. Mom worked the early shift in the store. Summer came, and they figured that an able-bodied teenager would give them some relief. I got those jobs. I did so well for them that they must have suggested to the woman who ran the Jewish lunchroom next door that I was a wonderful worker. (All those who have worked with me can pause here for laughter.) I became a Pearl Diver at Pearl's two days a week.

The work wasn't all that bad. It wasn't boring since there were three different jobs. In fact it was interesting, because it was an opportunity to learn about Judaism and kosher dietary rules. This augmented my knowledge that I got from going to school in South Shore. Since my dad would not tolerate any disrespect for others' beliefs, I was very open to absorbing all this neat stuff.

I wasn't quite as tolerant of another group of people I came in contact with, however. They were the men who inhabited the corner of 75th & Cottage Grove, where I hung out. Every time I hear the song "Bums on the Lawn," I think of those guys. Though we never abused them or did anything nasty, we didn't like them or give them money no matter how much they begged.

One day I wanted to go to the beach with the gang. It was a big deal; everyone was going. Unfortunately, it was Felix's day off. I begged and pleaded. I offered to come in the evening and do the job. To no avail, I was stuck. I wasn't happy. I was doing the morning portion (mom's) of the job, when Huey, one of the bums, came in. My dad always gave him day-old stuff, two bags full, for nothing. Well, on this day as I was putting his stuff in a bag, my dad inquired if Huey was there. He then went into the store and asked him if he would like to make some money. When the answer was affirmative, dad took him into the back by the sink. After being told what the porter's job entailed, he said he'd do it. Dad turned to me and said that I could go to the beach. I could have kissed Huey.

Dad also told me that if I made the 10:30 delivery, I could have the car. My cup runneth over. When I came back to do that, I thanked Huey again, and talked to him for a bit. I found out that he was retarded and couldn't see very well.

Keeping Our Heads on Straight

The following morning dad showed me what a good job Huey had done. He didn't say it, but if we had been competing, Huey would have beat me going away. To this day whenever they talk about jobs and mentally handicapped people, I remember standing there looking at the results of Huey's work.

Since that time when Huey would come in for day-old stuff, I would give him all the premium goodies. I would speak politely to him as he always had to me. And when I would encounter him on the corner, I would smile and ask after his health. Further, when he would ask, I never refused him the price of a pint of muscatel.

12600 S. TORRENCE AVE

I drove by 130th & Torrence for the next to the last time as the wife of an employee of the Ford Motor Company's Chicago Assembly Plant. My husband's co-workers were throwing a party, and I was invited. I saluted the white flag with the blue oval as I put my Escort into the slot next to Larry's Crown Vic. This is the second best spot in the lot. At one time even better than the plant manager's, and it will go to someone who has been vying for it since Larry said he was going to retire.

The lobby of the plant is Spartan. They build cars here and do not waste time or money on frills. I must call on the phone and have someone come and get me. Larry does. We go through the office area. I am introduced to the big brass, no frills in these offices either. Nobody wears a suit, not even the plant manager.

Larry and I get on a buggy to go to his department. As we drive by the 96's, I think back to the first time he and I did this. They were making the 67's. Larry was known in many departments, and everybody he introduced me to stopped what they were doing and stared at me. I told my mother this, and she immediately wanted to know what I had been wearing. I told her that we had come from Aunt Netty's funeral. She sighed with relief because she had given me this dark lavender suit to wear. She always fretted over my choice of clothes.

In the time that has passed between the 67's and the 96's, Larry and I have bought and paid for a house, reared and educated two children, and have a nice retirement package. Because of the employee stock plan, we have some of that, too. For all this, as I was going down Torrence Ave. to the parking lot that last day, I kept saying "thank you" over and over.

Well, they stared at me again that day. Mom would be proud, I'm wearing an outfit Carole O.K.'d. They asked me how I liked the idea of having Larry home all the time. I told them that I could hardly wait to have him all to myself.

At one point I was sitting by Larry's phone; it rang, I answered it. "Plant Engineering, Wozniak," I said. I even copied his rhythm. There was a pause.

"I must have the wrong number," the voice on the other end of the phone said.

"No, you have the right number, but the wrong Wozniak," I chortled and handed the phone to Larry's replacement.

☙

Lyn Wozniak—from Roselyn Kreher to Mrs. L. V. to WoZ— varies her name as she creates herself in a new image. She is a retired surgical nurse, scuba diver, devoted wife, and a two-mile swimmer.